PERENNIAL FLOWERS
FOR SMALL GARDENS

Pan Piper Small Garden Series
Editor: C. E. Lucas Phillips

PERENNIAL FLOWERS FOR SMALL GARDENS

PETER HUNT

A PAN ORIGINAL

Line drawings by
CYNTHIA HUNT

PAN BOOKS LTD: LONDON

First published 1965 by
PAN BOOKS LTD
8 Headfort Place, London, S.W.1

PRINTED IN ENGLAND BY
HAZELL WATSON AND VINEY LTD
AYLESBURY, BUCKS

To my wife who has helped me
to grow so many plants
and who has appreciated them all

CONTENTS

ILLUSTRATIONS IN PHOTOGRAVURE

ILLUSTRATIONS IN PHOTOGRAVURE

Pyrethrum 'Brenda'

Rudbeckia 'Autumn Glow'

Rodgersia aesculifolia

Sidalcea 'Rev. Page Roberts'

Primula viali

Sedum spectabile

Euphorbia epithymoides

All the photographs except those showing a section of an herbaceous border
and Russell lupins were taken by the
author and are his copyright

LINE DRAWINGS

CHAPTER I

THE USES OF HARDY PERENNIALS

BORDER FASHIONS – FOLIAGE – THE DWARFS
THE GIANTS

THIS book concerns the culture of those flowers known as
'hardy herbaceous perennials'. What are they?

They are the plants we loosely call 'border' plants; not
annuals, which have to be sown afresh each year and which die
after they have flowered; not biennials, which are sown one
year to flower the next and then die; not shrubs or trees, which
are hardy perennials, but not hardy *herbaceous* perennials; and
finally not bulbs.

What is left? Very many plants, most of which go on flowering each year for years and years, the stems which they produce
one season dying down at the end of the season and new ones
being produced the following season. A few are evergreen, and
these do not die down in quite the same way; their flower stems
die down, but there is left an evergreen crown from which
fresh flowering stems rise the following year.

The essential point, therefore, is that hardy herbaceous
perennials, with a few exceptions, lose all or nearly all their
top growth in winter, but remain alive below ground. A few
may need a little protection in winter in some places, but
this does not really detract from their general hardiness. They
are among the most useful of all plants, for they do not
require a great deal of attention: no more than many shrubs,

no more than most bulbs, probably less than annuals and biennials.

Border Fashions

In the small garden they may be used in many ways. The traditional way, although the tradition probably dates back less than a century, is to grow them in borders, usually called herbaceous borders. The death-knell of this charming feature has been sounded often over the last couple of decades, but it is a long time a'dying and is likely to be with us for many years to come, in one form or another. Indeed, there is no better way of displaying a varied selection of hardy perennials than in such a border, which is why they are often known under the alternative name of border plants. Although it is difficult to get away entirely from the general idea of the border, there have certainly been successful attempts to modify and adapt the concept of the large herbaceous border to make it more suitable for the smaller gardens of today and also to fit in as far as possible with modern ideas of labour-saving gardens.

Thus, there is growing interest in the 'mixed border' in which flowering shrubs, both evergreen and deciduous, are used to form a permanent framework to the border, giving it a certain form and interest during the winter months, adding their quota of colour during the spring, summer and autumn. Bulbs, annuals and even bedding plants may find a place in such a mixed border, thus ensuring that the available space is used to the best advantage, to grow a diverse range of plants, instead of confining it to hardy herbaceous perennials alone.

Mr Alan Bloom, the hardy plant nurseryman, of Bressingham, Norfolk, has done much to popularise through his writings and broadcasts both the 'midget' border, 4 or 5 ft wide, in which plants from about 6 in to $2\frac{1}{2}$ ft may well be displayed, and the double-sided border, often called the 'island' or 'walk-round' border.

The midget border, admirably suited to the small garden,

does tend to limit a little the plants which may be grown, since many border plants grow well over $2\frac{1}{2}$ ft. But there is still a surprising number which come within the height range and it is possible to plan such a border to give colour and interest over a long period and its scale generally fits in better with the smaller garden.

The double-sided border gets away from the generally accepted idea of having the border backed by a hedge, fence, wall or pergola, the tallest plants at the back, sloping down to dwarf plants at the front. Instead, in the double-sided border, the taller plants are placed in the centre and shorter plants on each side of them. There is great scope for planting in such a border and, because it cannot all be seen at once, there is usually an element of mystery, of surprise.

So much for the concept of borders. Details of planning, preparing and planting them are discussed in Chapter II. But there are other ways of growing hardy perennials. They may, for instance, be grown in isolated groups, consisting of one or more plants, either of one species or variety, or of several species or varieties in the same genus. There are all sorts of odd spots in the garden, a few feet square, where this plan may be adopted. The plants flowering in winter or spring are well suited for growing in this way as they are generally too early in flower to be accommodated in the border proper, which is more of a May-to-October feature.

Groups of hellebores, of which the best known are the Christmas and Lenten Roses, may be planted in those sometimes difficult shady spots and left alone to increase slowly year after year, requiring little attention and flowering prolifically. The early leopard's banes (doronicums) are often in flower in March, when many of the border plants are only just beginning to show signs of life. These, too, may be planted under trees in large groups to brighten the March days with their large yellow daisies. The later doronicums may well be planted in the border to start the season.

Numerous other ways of employing herbaceous flowers present themselves, for their diversity is immense. Thus the Michaelmas daisies go excellently in the shrub border. In woodland setting, or in any part of the small garden not too heavily overhung, we may enjoy the wistful bleeding heart, the campanulas, whose airy bells will light up the darkest corner, the Japanese anemones, the familiar foxglove, the arching arms of Solomon's seal and the three-petalled trillium.

For very dry soils, especially sandy ones, we have the azalea-like brilliance of the new alstroemerias, the bold garden yarrows (Achillea), the cornflower-like Cupid's dart (Catananche), the big brothers of the chamomile (Anthemis), the gay gaillardia, the fleshy-leaved sedums and the bristly top-knots of sea holly and globe thistle.

For the opposite sort of soil we have at our disposal several moisture-loving perennials, the phlox, kingcups, day lilies, the old purple loosestrife, together with several that revel even in boggy ground, among which are to be numbered some of our loveliest plants, including the plumed astilbe, the candelabra primulas and the superlative Japanese irises.

Foliage

Some plants are valued as much for their foliage as for their flowers and these, too, may often be seen to the best advantage if they are isolated. Examples which come to mind are the acanthus, stately plants with handsomely cut leaves, beloved of Greek sculptors of old, and tall stems of interesting flowers. Grown by themselves they seem to gain a good deal; in the border their effect is partly lost.

Hostas, or plantain-lilies, excellent plants for partial shade under trees, with beautiful leaves, bluish-green or variegated with cream or white, according to species and variety, also look their best when grown in isolated masses.

The hardy geraniums (cranesbills), useful border plants

though they are, may be planted in bold masses.[1] The most useful for this purpose is *Geranium endressii* because it produces its pink flowers over such a long period, from June to October, or even into November if they are not spoiled by the first severe frosts. The plant grows about 15 in tall and will thrive happily in full sun or partial shade, rapidly making extensive but not invasive clumps. There are varieties showing slight colour variations. This useful geranium may be planted by itself or in company with other hardy geraniums, of which there are many with attractive flowers in various colours, ranging in height from the few inches of the kinds usually grown on rock gardens to the nearly 3 ft of the taller kinds. None flowers over such a long period as *G. endressii*, but all are interesting and their foliage is pleasant and not untidy after the flowers have faded and been cut off. There are many other plants which lend themselves to being grown in this way; the thing to do is to experiment.

The Dwarfs

Mention of the hardy geraniums grown on rock gardens leads me to other plants which are normally grown there or on dry walls. There is no reason why the alpine gardener should have the monopoly of the dwarfer plants. Many of them are perfectly easy hardy perennials, which will grow as well on the flat as on the slopes of the rock garden, particularly if the soil is well drained. Such plants as aubrietas, alyssums, the charming *Anemone pulsatilla*, the dwarf achilleas or garden yarrows, the taller alpine gentians such as *G. septemfida*, the alpine pinks, except the very dwarf kinds, and a number of other plants may be grown.

Not long ago we raised about two hundred pinks from seed sent by a friend, collected from good varieties. As may be

[1] Not to be confused with the so-called 'Geraniums' used for bedding-out in public parks; these are properly pelargoniums and are not hardy.

expected they were a mixed lot, but there was scarcely one among them which was not worth growing. The colour variation in the pink to crimson range was wide, many of the flowers had attractive darker 'zones' or rings in their centres, there were one or two white-flowered kinds, and there was a height range from about 4 or 5 in to a foot or so. Having such a large number we were able to make lavish plantings, using them for edging, for planting on a sunny bank, between the cracks in paving stones and in all sorts of odd corners.

The cracks between paving stones, some narrow, but capable of being widened, some wider already, are other places where certain hardy perennials may be grown. The dwarf, less rampant kinds, which make neat clumps are best for this purpose. Some decent soil packed into the cracks or into spaces made by removing the odd stone here and there, is all they need.

Once they have settled in their roots spread about happily below the paving stones where the soil is always cool and moist. They also appreciate having their top growth baked by whatever sun we have, gaining something from the heat stored by and reflected by the paving stones. Such plants as pinks, aubrietas, alyssums, thrifts, do well there and there are many others which may be tried. It is best, of course, to choose positions out of the way of footsteps.

The Giants

By contrast with these dwarf perennials, there are the really tall ones which may make well over 6 ft of growth in a single season, some even reaching 8 ft when they are well grown. They may be too tall for the border proper in the small garden but they may have a use in providing a temporary, leafy, flowering screen.

Among such plants are the perennial sunflowers, the 'plume poppy' (*Macleaya cordata*), the taller rudbeckias and *Senecio tanguticus*, all of which grow rapidly and flower late. They should all reach 6 ft or more in good soil and where the site is not exposed. They are leafy enough to provide some sort of a screen, certainly to screen one part of the garden from another, perhaps while a hedge is growing up.

CHAPTER II

MAKING AND MAINTAINING THE BORDER

PLANNING – PREPARING – PLANTING – CARING

IN this chapter we shall discuss the making of an herbaceous border as such, but what I have to say is also applicable to other places than the formal border where perennials are to be grown. In my small space I am not able to deal as I should wish with the characteristics of different soils, their management and garden operations generally. Readers not already familiar with these basic matters are referred to *The Small Garden*, by the editor of this Pan series. I would take this opportunity, however, of emphasising that, except for bog-loving plants, the first requirement of all gardening success is good drainage.

Before making any kind of plan, it is vital to study the factors of the piece of ground at your disposal. The nature of your soil – whether sandy, clay, chalk or fat loam – may in the first place determine what you may or may not grow. The aspect of your garden may affect their selection no less.

In general, but with important exceptions, border plants prefer a situation in full sun, not overhung by trees, but a certain amount of oblique shade is acceptable. A border that faces more or less south holds out the best hopes of reward. North-facing borders or beds (having a wall, hedge or fence behind them) present their special problem, but the shade lovers then may have a large claim on your space. I have mentioned several of these in one of the sections of Chapter V.

Planning

Planning the layout of the border is a pleasant task for the fireside on a winter's evening, when outdoor gardening is a matter of memories and of hopes for the future. By then the nurserymen's catalogues will have arrived, full of illustrations, some plain, some coloured, to set the gardener dreaming of a garden full of flowers from early spring to late autumn, unharmed by the vagaries of the British weather, untouched by pests, enlivened by well-behaved birds and butterflies. As the late gardener-poet Victoria Sackville-West said in her poem *The Garden*:

> 'We dream our dreams.
> What should we be, without our fabulous flowers?
> The gardener dreams his special own alloy
> Of possible and the impossible.'

To come down to earth, as all gardeners should after their daydreams, planning uses for hardy herbaceous plants is not difficult. The newcomer to gardening may like to follow a few simple 'rules', but, like most rules, they are made to be broken and broken they will be as experience is gained.

As far as planning a border is concerned the main thing is to plan it thoroughly on paper first. A large piece of squared paper, pinned to a board, is useful but not absolutely essential. Its main virtue is that it helps one to draw out the proposed border to scale after jotting down any necessary measurements taken on the site itself. It is worth marking on the plan any fixed features such as existing trees which are to remain, fences, hedges, etc., and also the compass points.

The outline of the border may then be drawn in as accurately to scale as possible, remembering that if you are working to a scale of $\frac{1}{2}$ in = 1 ft then an error of, say, $\frac{1}{2}$ in on the plan is magnified to 1 ft on the site, which may mean that all your proposed planting sites will be so much out.

Before marking in the positions of any plants it is well worth going to the trouble of getting some gummed and coloured paper from the stationers. The colours need be no more than primary ones. After making a selection of plants, using the descriptions in Chapter V as a guide, cut up these gummed papers into pieces about $1\frac{1}{2}$ in square to represent a group of three plants. This is usually a sufficiently large group for the smaller borders which are suitable for smaller gardens.

In large borders it is often necessary to plant in groups of five to get the necessary bold effect. Mark on the pieces of paper of appropriate colour the names of the plants, their heights and their flowering seasons. Make the selection so that there is something of interest in the border from April to October or early November, when the last of the Michaelmas daisies goes over.

In the small border this is not too easy, as, unless the choice is made carefully, there may be periods when there are large patches without colour. In the early stages while the border is new this can be overcome by using the temporary colour provided by bedding plants, hardy annuals and bulbs, but this becomes less possible as the plants within the groups spread to touch each other and the groups themselves join up.

You may find it better, in fact, if the border is to be only 20–30 ft long, to leave out any plants that flower before late May, when the columbines and some other plants are at their best. There *are* hardy plants which will give a good deal of colour earlier, but they may well be grown elsewhere than in the border, perhaps in association with the spring-flowering bulbs. This means that it will be possible to concentrate your display over a shorter period, with consequently less danger of finding blank spots.

The choice made (and there is plenty from which to choose in Chapter V), the coloured papers marked up, the plan drawn to scale, the fitting in of groups of plants can then begin. It would be a lucky, or knowledgeable, gardener who hit on the perfect plan right away. Usually the pieces of paper have to be shuffled around on the plan until a satisfactory compromise has been reached, taking into account the factors of colour, height and flowering period.

Start by fitting in the taller plants first; those of $3\frac{1}{2}$–4 ft in height and upwards. In one-sided borders, those backed by a fence, hedge, wall or pergola, these taller plants will in general be placed at the back, those 2–$3\frac{1}{2}$ ft tall in front of them, and the dwarf plants, from 6–9 in tall to going on for 2 ft tall, at the front. If the border is a two-sided one, an 'island' or 'walk-round' border, then the tall plants will form a spine down the centre and plants of diminishing height will be set on either side of them.

These, however, are among the 'rules' mentioned earlier which will inevitably be broken. In fact, it is best to break the rule now and again, otherwise it is possible to produce an effect that is altogether too formal, with even steps in height from back to front or from centre to edges. And formality is the last thing one should wish to introduce in a feature of this kind.

Occasionally, therefore, when formality appears to be creeping in, break up the line by bringing forward a group of taller plants. Sometimes a group which might otherwise be planted in the centre of the border may be brought almost to the front. But a point to beware of here is not to bring forward plants which have a short flowering season, otherwise there may be an ugly gap at the front over a long period. Instead, choose a plant which will produce some flowers at least through most of the summer.

Once a satisfactory compromise has been reached, the pieces of paper may be gummed down in their places on the plan and the order can be sent into the nurseryman. Get the order in as quickly as possible, otherwise there may be exasperating delays in receiving the plants. As with many things, it is very much a matter of 'first come, first served' and if your order is received late it may be that spring is well advanced before the plants arrive.

Most plants may safely be planted in the autumn so that, if time can be found to plan the border in the summer, and to get the ground ready by October or November, the order may be sent in during the summer for autumn delivery. Except for a few plants, and the exceptions are noted in Chapter V, the planting season extends from late October to April, provided the weather is suitable and the ground is not frozen, covered with snow, or water-logged.

Preparing

It is possible to grow hardy plants simply by digging a hole large enough to take the roots, popping the plant in, firming the soil and going away to await developments. There will be developments and, most hardy plants being good-tempered and able to put up with a good deal of neglect, the plant will grow and flower. But no one would recommend this as a method and I certainly do not. The plant will be growing in the same place for several years, indeed, paeonies are likely to be still flourishing above ground after you are beneath it.

I am not a fanatic about deep digging, however great its virtues may be; a 'disc' which may slip again and reduce me to gardening on hands and knees, prevents this. In any case, were I to try to dig more than one spit deep on my present soil, I should find a pneumatic drill a more useful tool than a spade, as the solid chalk is not far below the surface. Even on the soil of an earlier garden it was impracticable to dig too deeply, for doing so meant turning up large lumps of blue clay.

But I do believe in good general cultivation, by which I mean proper digging over the whole of the site, the removal of

the larger pieces of builder's rubble such as bricks, tiles, lumps
of concrete tipped out of the mixer at the end of the day and
eventually buried, together with all possible perennial weeds.
The *annual* weeds may well be dug in, provided they are well
below the surface, since they will rot down quite quickly to add
to the plant food in the soil. But such frightful perennial weeds
as bell-bind (the convolvulus of our hedgerows), couch grass,
docks, perennial nettles, dandelions and thistles, should be
sought for diligently and removed and burnt. Their plant-ash
may be returned to the soil later to provide a little extra potash.

As far as the herbaceous border is concerned, the first two
weeds mentioned are by far the worst. The remainder may
usually be removed fairly easily from among the plants, either
in their young stages or later when they have developed enough
top-hamper to enable one to get a good grasp and pull, although a preliminary loosening with a border fork is often
necessary to avoid breaking the deep tap roots. But once bell-
bind (or bindweed to some people) and couch grass get a hold
in the border, as they will quickly do unless every tiny fragment
is removed from the soil when it is being cultivated, there is
little one can do afterwards but dig up the plants and clean the
ground again, properly this time.

Worst of all, though, is having to clean the plants themselves.
To remove every piece of couch grass or convolvulus from a
large clump of Michaelmas daisies is a task to daunt Hercules,
not because of the strength required, but the patience needed.
I have had to do this job on more than one occasion and have
found that there is sometimes nothing to do but to split the
clump up into small pieces, no bigger than one's fist and then
gently tease out each piece of weed root, making sure that it
does not break in so doing.

When the plant has been growing in heavy clay the task
becomes even harder and then the only way is to wash off as
much of the clay as possible before removing the weed roots.
This is a task which on a cold winter's day can only be com-

pared with picking brussels sprouts on a commercial scale.

Heed, therefore, the dire warning and remove every piece of weed root from your border before you plant. If necessary, if it is very weedy, dig the soil over in the spring and clean it up as much as possible, then leave it fallow for the summer. This will give any weeds which have been missed an opportunity to grow during the summer (and you may be certain that they will), so that you can see where they are. Many of them may be removed during the summer, digging down until their origin is found, probably a small piece of root, an inch or two long, often buried below the level to which the digging was done (an argument, of course, for really deep digging). A final forking over may be necessary in the autumn before planting is done.

Most 'ordinary' garden soils, provided they have not been continuously cropped without any plant foods being returned to them, are reasonably fertile and the act of cultivation, by allowing air to get into the soil, rain to penetrate more easily, will release a good deal of their fertility, making foods available to the plants. But it is still best to add something to the soil while digging is being carried out and on poor soils it is essential.

What to add is another matter. Years ago, when horses were more common than mechanical horse-power, the answer was easy, even if one lived in a town. If you are still able to get good animal manure, particularly cow manure, you are mad not to use it. Dig it well in, mixing it with the soil at the bottom of the top spit, at the rate of five or six spadefuls to the square yard.

Nowadays, however, it is mainly on home-made, manureless compost, that we must rely, and when well-made it is not to be despised. This is no place to describe the making of a compost-heap. I can only say that one of the first jobs on taking over a new garden, and one which should go on all the time is to provide a reasonably continuous supply of material, for digging in from autumn to spring, for mulching plants of all kinds at other times.

One can never have too much, but it is surprising how much can be made, even in the small garden, especially if the weeds, dead flowers, grass-cuttings, soft hedge trimmings and other waste plant material are supplemented with kitchen waste. Another excellent material for digging in, not too near the top, is chopped-up turf, especially in sandy soils.

Years ago, when we lived in the Midlands on the outskirts of a town which boasted several breweries, we were able to buy spent hops, the residues of the process of brewing, excellent material for digging into the soil in large quantities to rot down. It is not so easy to get hold of nowadays, but if you are lucky enough to have a source of supply, don't fail to make us of it.

More easily obtained are bales of straw. These may be composted quite quickly by opening them up, soaking them thoroughly and assisting the process of decay by scattering sulphate of ammonia on them. This rotted straw is a valuable plant food.

Peat, too, is readily obtainable, either in very dry bales or in moist sacks. It does not contain a great deal of plant food in itself, but it is most useful on any type of soil, for digging in or as a surface mulch. Bales must be broken down first and then thoroughly moistened, or the bale may be left out in the rain for some weeks to enable it to soak up as much moisture as possible. If you are in a hurry make a hole in the bale and put the hose in and allow it to trickle *gently* for some hours.

Peat may be dug in liberally; it will considerably improve the texture of clay soils by opening them up and enabling air to penetrate more easily. On sandy soils it helps to improve the water-retaining properties and also helps the soil to retain plant foods which might otherwise be washed out easily. On chalk soils it helps to counteract to some extent the effects of the chalk, in rendering certain plant foods unavailable, but it is probably more useful as a surface mulch, applied each spring, thus helping to build up fertility over a long period. On other soils peat may be used in this way or may be dug in during the autumn or spring.

I have had very good results with a seaweed manure. This consists, I think, of dried and powdered seaweeds to which have been added inorganic fertilisers to produce what is known as a 'complete fertiliser'. A few ounces of this per square yard worked into the top spit of soil before planting, seems to be very effective. I also use it in the planting soil at the rate of a handful per bucket.

In addition to these plant foods, which are mainly organic there are, of course, the so-called 'artificials' or inorganic fertilisers. These are invaluable, provided the dosage is not overdone, but unfortunately they do nothing to improve the *texture* of the soil, which often does need improving. The thing to do is use them wisely, in conjunction with such organics as manure, peat, compost, spent hops, etc. They are also invaluable for use in late spring and summer, either as dry top-dressings, watered into the soil, or in liquid form. Some firms put up balanced 'flower fertilisers' and these are worth having as they have been specially blended for the purpose. Use these at the rates recommended by the manufacturers; don't be tempted to double the rates in the hope of getting results twice as good for things don't work out that way.

Planting

Before planting is done the plan made on paper has to be transferred to the actual site. Be as accurate as possible when doing this, as otherwise you may get to the end of the border, and find either that you have plants left over or that you haven't enough to go round.

So divide the site up into squares corresponding with those on the plan, using pegs alone or pegs and cords. The planting positions may be marked inside the squares with labels on which are written the plant names. This may sound an unnecessary refinement, but it does avoid too much trampling backwards and forwards.

Another way is to place the plants in position in the squares before starting, but the objection to this is that they may suffer on a sunny, windy day, their roots shrivelling before they are covered with soil. Most of the plants are tough enough to put up with this, but there is no point in checking them unnecessarily. Why pay good money for plants and then neglect them?

As mentioned earlier in this chapter, the planting season is a long one in most years. It is quite possible to plant in wet weather, when heavy soils are 'claggy' and pick up on the boots. But if they are in this condition it is best to put boards down on the soil and walk on these rather than on the ground, to avoid consolidating it too much and thus forcing out the air which you have been able to get into the soil by proper digging.

The soil will probably be too wet and sticky to use round the plants when planting, so, if you garden on these heavy soils, it helps to prepare a load of special planting soil earlier in the season before the wet weather sets in. This can consist mainly of ordinary, dryish garden soil, plus a fair amount of leaf-mould and peat or compost and peat. Old potting compost is a useful addition as it contains both sand and peat. Spent mushroom compost is also excellent if you can get it from a reliable source. Two or three handfuls of coarse bonemeal added to each barrow-load will provide extra food for the plants as they are settling down. This planting soil should be kept under cover, either in a shed or under a sheet of corrugated iron or, perhaps, a sheet of heavy plastic held down with bricks, until it is needed.

Planting is not difficult. On heavy soils in particular it is essential not to plant too deeply otherwise water may collect in the crown of the plant and set up rot. Always make a planting hole large enough to take the roots spread out properly rather than squashed up together. Make sure the soil round the plants is properly firmed, using the knuckles where small plants are concerned, the boot to firm round larger ones. It is at this point that previously prepared planting soil comes in useful.

When planting has been completed, take an early opportunity of raking the soil surface over to remove footmarks, especially on heavy soils. This is not merely for the sake of tidiness, but to prevent rainwater collecting in puddles and eventually forming a hard surface crust which tends to keep air out of the soil. After periods of frost it may be necessary to look over the border and refirm any plants which have been heaved out of the soil. This sometimes happens to small specimens.

If plants arrive from the nursery when it is impossible to plant them, remove them from their wrappings and keep them in a cool but frost-proof shed or outhouse until they can be planted. Keep the wrapping round the roots but not round any top growth, otherwise this will become pale and thin and spindly and, if the temperature is too high, it may become mouldy.

A good method if the bad weather is likely to be prolonged is to set the plants temporarily in deep boxes, pots or other containers, using some of the planting soil mentioned above. They can then be kept outdoors in a sheltered place.

Alternatively, if the soil is not frost-bound, the plants may be heeled-in, temporarily – a simple matter of making a hole or slit in the soil and putting the roots in and refirming. But if the soil is frost-bound or snow-covered, heeling-in is also impossible, and the method of temporary planting in boxes then comes in useful.

Caring

Staking. Plants make rapid growth as the spring advances and by early May the shoots of many of them may be a foot or so tall. This is the time to start staking, otherwise much damage may be caused by high winds in late spring and early summer.

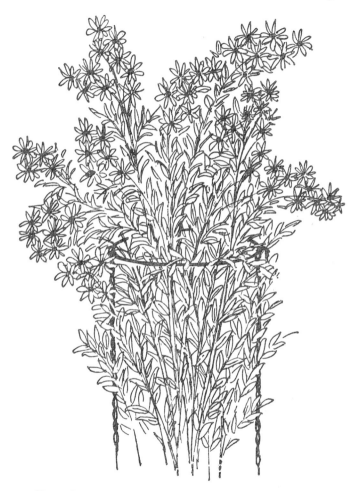

FIG. 1. The 'Bracknell' plant support is ideal for those plants
which make large clumps. Made with legs of various heights
and with circles of various diameters, they are almost hidden by
leafy plants. No tying is needed

A good many plants need not be staked at all, except, perhaps, in very exposed gardens. A good many others can only be described as somewhat floppy in growth and these need some support in the form of twiggy sticks thrust into the ground round the individual plants or groups. Others, of upright, spiky growths, such as delphiniums and lupins, are better off with a separate stake or stout cane for each spike.

Ideally, staking should be unobtrusive, since nobody wants a border in which the main feature is a forest of canes or twigs. But after May they are hidden by the growth of the plants. Large clusters, such as those of Michaelmas daisies and other daisies, need a fair amount of staking to stop them from flopping about too much. The 'Bracknell Plant Supports' are useful for this purpose. These are stout wire rings made in various diameters up to 10 in, with legs up to 5 ft long, which may be used to encircle the plant and hold it upright. After a short while these are hardly noticeable, as the foliage hides them.

Thinning. A good many hardy herbaceous plants produce large numbers of stems and, if these are left unthinned, the flowers are often small and untypical of the plant. Thinning is not necessary with newly-planted specimens, but is often needed after they have been growing in the same place for a couple of years and have made fairly extensive clumps. The daisy-flowered plants, particularly Michaelmas asters, also delphiniums and phloxes, do far better if they are thinned, responding by producing stronger stems and larger flowers.

The time to do this is during May and early June and, drastic though it sounds, up to half the shoots may be removed to advantage. First remove all weak shoots, then thin shoots mainly from the centre of the plant, cutting them right down to the ground. The shoots that remain will have better access to light and air.

Deadheading. This means the removal of spent flowers and is a job which ought to be attended to regularly throughout the flowering season. The herbaceous border is planned to be admired and an array of tatty seed pods does not improve its looks. Carry a pair of secateurs or garden scissors all the time and snip off the dead and dying flower-heads as soon as they are seen. This will effectively prevent the plants from concentrating their energies on developing seed and, furthermore, it often results in their developing side-shoots from farther down the stem which will produce flowers later in the season, thus prolonging the colour in the border.

Lupins and delphiniums are good examples; if their flower stems are cut down as soon as the flowers have faded they will usually develop secondary spikes to flower in late summer and autumn. These will not be so large and bold as the early spikes but they are nevertheless welcome.

Some plants, especially the hardy geraniums (cranesbills) and aubrietas, sometimes used for edging borders, are best treated by clipping them over with shears. Many of the geraniums will flower again, the aubrietas will not, but the clipping will, at any rate, remove unsightly dead flowers and will encourage the formation of new flowering growth for the following season.

Annual Maintenance. Annual maintenance of the border is undertaken at two seasons, autumn and spring. By the time November has come most of the border flowers will be over; those that remain are the last of the late Michaelmas daisies and, here and there, a few flowers on plants which gave their main display weeks or even months earlier. Most of them are looking bedraggled, battered by the equinoctial gales, their stems for the most part brown and dry.

This is the time to go over the border cutting down plants and generally tidying up. All the dead and dying stems should be cut down close to the ground with secateurs or sharp knife. It is dangerous to leave short lengths of stem protruding from the crown of the plant because these become hard and woody and may cause nasty injuries when one is working among the plants in later years.

This is the time, too, for forking between the plants, not deeply, lest roots near the surface are damaged, but pricking the soil over, letting in air, removing weeds and plant rubbish. Autumn or early winter is also the time to apply an annual dressing of well-rotted compost, to help the plants to build up their strength for the coming season. This may be lightly forked or dug into the soil, again avoiding roots as far as possible.

A few plants may need a little winter protection. Fox-tail lilies (eremurus) need the protection of a covering of bracken or dry peat over their crowns. In cold districts or in exposed gardens, red hot pokers (kniphofias) may be protected by surrounding them with dry leaves held in place with wire netting.

In the spring such protective coverings may be removed and the soil between the plants again pricked over to remove the surface crust which often forms after the winter's rains. But, before doing this, scatter a dressing of a general flower fertiliser at the rate recommended by the manufacturers on the soil round the plants, avoiding the leaves. Take this opportunity of removing any weeds.

CHAPTER III

PROPAGATING YOUR OWN PLANTS

BY DIVISION – BY SEED – BY STEM CUTTINGS – BY ROOT
CUTTINGS

MUCH of the pleasure in gardening is derived from
propagating one's own plants. There is a great deal of
satisfaction in looking at a plant or a bed or border of plants
and thinking 'all my own work'. The cutting taken a year ago is
now a substantial plant; what was once a tiny seedling is now a
large clump; the small piece with a few leaves and roots, taken
from a friend's plant, is now the pride of the border.

There are four principal methods of increasing one's stock:
by division, by seed, by stem cuttings and by root cuttings.

By Division

This is the easiest of all methods and the great majority of
border plants may be so propagated. It is merely a question of
digging up the clumps, splitting them up into smaller pieces
and replanting them.

Sometimes it is not even necessary to dig up the clump. All
our present stock of *Geranium endressii*, amounting to a score or
more of plants, was obtained when we moved from one garden
to another by taking a sharp spade and chopping round a clump,
which was then about $1\frac{1}{2}$ ft in diameter, removing pieces a few
inches across from all round the plant. This was done in late

February. By June the pieces were in flower and had already made good plants. By April the original plant in the old garden showed no signs of anything having been removed from it at all. One cannot do this with every border plant, but it does serve to illustrate how easy the operation can be.

Most of the hardy herbaceous perennials which make clumps may be divided almost at any time from late autumn to early spring when the weather is suitable. Some, however, you must divide in spring; these include pyrethrums, scabious, Shasta daisies, and the amellus species of perennial asters. Bearded irises and polyanthus ought to be divided as soon as they have finished flowering.

When dividing border plants, it does pay to dig them up first, simply because they are so prolific in growth, sending up such a mass of flowering stems, that they practically flower themselves to death. Certainly they start to die in the centre after a few years and it is not uncommon to find, when one comes to dig up an old clump, that much of the centre consists of a mass of woody material of little value, all the new growth coming from the perimeter. It is these outside pieces which should be replanted in the border. The worn-out centre portion is best cremated.

How the division of the clumps should be carried out depends very much on the type of growth that the plant has made. Some make such a close matted tangle that, in heavy soils especially, the only practicable way is to chop the whole clump up with a sharp spade or edging iron. A certain amount of damage will be done inevitably, but if the work is done during the dormant season, as it usually is, then the divisions will soon recover. Examples are hostas, day lilies, Siberian irises and tradescantias, which have very tough roots.

Somewhat easier to deal with are those plants which make a reasonably loose mass of growth, even though this may appear to be a complete tangle when dug up. Plants such as these may usually be divided by placing two garden forks in the clump back to back and waggling them back and forth until the clump falls apart into several pieces. Examples are Michaelmas daisies, golden rod, anthemis and artemisias. Easier still are those plants, such as polyanthus, which can be pulled apart

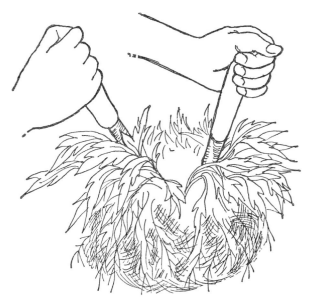

FIG. 2. Many clump-forming herbaceous plants may be easily divided by using two hand-forks. Others may be pulled apart, and some are so tough that they must be chopped up with the spade

with the hands, and those which may be divided with no more equipment than a sharp old kitchen knife.

When you are dividing, try to remove any weed roots and shoots which you come across. Badly weed-infested clumps may have to be split up into quite small pieces and each of these washed in running water to remove the soil before the weeds can be removed. Replant all divisions as soon as possible. If delay is unavoidable, cover them with damp sacks or heel them in temporarily.

This process of division should be carried out regularly every three or four years to all plants that make wide-spreading thickets, such as Michaelmas daisies and heleniums. If your border is of baronial proportions, do a part of it each year.

Growing from Seed

Growing from seed is an interesting and rewarding occupation provided you have enough patience and a certain amount of discrimination. The patience is necessary because, although your seedlings will flower the year following sowing, or even in the year they are sown, it may be another year before you have a plant of decent size.

The discrimination is needed when you are dealing with such plants as lupins and delphiniums, complex hybrids which do not come true from seed. A fair proportion of the plants raised from seed of these and of a number of other plants of a like nature, will not be worth keeping. In such cases, allow the seedlings to flower and immediately discard all that are displeasing.

This is not necessarily to say that dwarf forms should be discarded; it is just possible that you may find among your seedlings a plant which grows to half the height or less than it should. This might be a useful addition to the range. Double forms of plants which are normally single-flowered occasionally turn up and these, too, may be worth keeping.

Even when plants do come true from seed it is worth keeping an eye on all the seedlings as they come into flower. You may possibly find a colour variation, perhaps pale sulphur yellow instead of golden yellow, perhaps deep red instead of pink. Many good varieties have been raised by accident and we owe their existence to the sharp eyes of gardeners, both professional and amateur, who have spotted the odd man out in a bed of seedlings, realised its worth and built up a stock by propagating from it vegetatively, that is, by division or by taking cuttings.

This is one of the excitements of gardening, the hope that something better or something different may turn up unexpectedly. At the time of writing I have a batch of about fifty seedlings of that delightful 'Greek mallow', *Sidalcea*, which is just coming into flower. The seedlings were taken from good named varieties and already show quite a wide variation of colour in the pink-red range, as well as variation in height. There is nothing really spectacular yet – I don't suppose there will be – but so far it looks as though all of them will be worth growing on. Likewise, a batch of columbines of the 'Giant McKana Strain' yielded plants in a delightful range of pastel shades and other colours, the flowers having very long spurs that are a feature of this strain. Again, all worth growing on.

Other examples of border plants that can be easily raised from seed are: the beautiful modern forms of alstroemeria (the only way to raise them), day lilies, campanulas, polyanthus and many others of the primrose family, erigeron, dittany (dictamnus), pinks, stachys, aubrieta, geum, foxglove.

Under Glass. Seeds of hardy herbaceous perennials may be sown under glass or outdoors. It is worth adopting both methods if you have time, as it gives you two chances. However, as the greenhouse sowing is done in spring, a very busy period, when annuals, half-hardy and hardy and vegetables are all clamouring to be sown, many gardeners prefer to give this period a miss as far as hardy border plants are concerned and wait until June, when they sow outdoors. None the less, there are certain sorts that it is almost essential to sow in spring; these include delphiniums, lupins, columbines, anthemis and coreopsis.

Personally, if I can find the time, I like to make a sowing under glass in the spring, although it is usually in the cold frame, the greenhouse normally being full. The advantages of sowing in pots, pans or boxes in the greenhouse or frame are that it is easier to keep an eye on the plants, there is less weeding to be done, and the seedlings have longer to develop into plants of reasonable size, which may usually be planted out in their flowering quarters in the autumn. Many of these, too, will flower in their first summer, often late, admittedly, but it is then possible to start discarding the poor ones or, where mixed colours are being grown, sorting them out into colour groups for planting in the border later.

Sowing in pots, boxes, etc., is done in John Innes Seed Compost or one of the modern soilless composts. Exposure to extremes of weather will hasten germination, so place the containers outdoors for two or three weeks, preferably in a frame from which the light has been removed. Then bring the boxes into the greenhouse or place them in a closed frame, cover them with sheets of glass and brown paper and germination should take place quite quickly.

Examine the boxes each day, turning the glass so that the condensation drips do not drop on to the soil. As soon as the seeds have germinated, remove the glass and paper and give the seedlings plenty of air and light. The plants are hardy and do not need any coddling. Don't wait until they are all through before removing the glass and paper; it is quite possible that more seeds will germinate afterwards. Germination is sometimes very erratic and may take place over a period of several weeks.

Keep them well watered and, when they are large enough, prick them out into deeper boxes or, if you have only a few, into individual pots, of John Innes Potting Compost or a suitable soilless potting compost. If the greenhouse is cool enough, they may be kept there for a while, but I prefer to grow them on in the cold frame, leaving the lights off except in very severe weather. They may later be planted out in rows in a sheltered nursery bed, but must be kept weeded.

A better method, where not too many seedlings are involved,

is to make a rough frame in an odd corner, either using planks nailed to pegs driven into the soil, or loose bricks. This can be of any convenient size, but the larger the better, and about a foot deep. After forking over the garden soil, I usually put a 2-in layer of moist peat at the bottom of the frame and then fill up with a mixture of garden soil, moist peat and sand, to within a couple of inches of the top, firming the mixture as the frame is filled.

The seedlings are set out in this, some 4–6 in apart, and grown here until they are set out in their flowering quarters in the autumn or early winter. Construct the frame in a light place but out of direct sunshine, otherwise the soil dries up quite quickly and must then be watered frequently. The plants make rapid headway and excellent root systems in a frame such as this.

Another method is to grow the seedlings in pots, which are then plunged to their rims in a frame filled with moist peat. The only disadvantage here is that the plants root through the drainage hole into the moist peat, find this so much to their liking that they make widespread root systems and it is consequently difficult to get them out of the pots without damaging some of the roots, which is a pity.

In the Open. Sowing in the open ground in June is a practicable proposition. The best place to do it is in the kitchen garden, where the soil is usually reasonably rich and an odd corner can usually be found. The seed is sown thinly in rows 6 or 8 in apart, the drills shallow, usually no more than $\frac{1}{4}$ in deep, unless the seeds are very large, and very few are. In dry weather water the drills the night before sowing.

Germination is usually quite rapid and, however thinly one sows, the seedlings usually come up too close together. This means they must be transplanted on to another bed when they are large enough to handle without damage, which is usually early in July. There they may be set out 6 to 9 in apart, according to their height, in rows a foot apart. Always plant with a trowel, not a dibber.

In hot weather the plants may need a good deal of attention until they get a root-hold, but this can be minimised by digging them up carefully when transplanting is being done, keeping as much soil round the roots as possible and having watered them before lifting. Dig up a few at a time only and get them back into their new bed as quickly as possible. On no account allow the roots to dry out. Moist peat liberally dug into the top few inches of the nursery bed will do much to prevent undue flagging in hot weather and enable the plants to settle down quickly.

The main attention from then on will be keeping down the annual weeds by running the hoe down the rows and between the plants. The seedlings may be planted out in their flowering quarters in the autumn or winter, but will come to no harm if this job has to wait until the spring.

By Stem Cuttings

A few perennials may be propagated by cuttings. This is an important method for delphiniums and lupins, because seedlings do not come true to their parents and because division, though possible, does not produce the best plants.

The cuttings are taken early in the spring before growth is too far advanced, choosing shoots 3 or 4 in long and either cutting them away from the crown with a small piece of the crown attached, or severing them immediately below a joint, using a very sharp knife or mounted razor-blade. Insert the cuttings, as close together as you like, in pans or pots of compost made up of one part loam, two peat and three sharp, horticultural sand. Put them in a closed propagating frame, but some ventilation is usually necessary otherwise there is a great risk of the cuttings failing through damping-off disease. When they have rooted they should be potted on individually into small pots of John Innes Potting Compost (or soilless potting compost) and given plenty of light and air. By late May they should be hardened off sufficiently for them to be planted out in the open ground in a nursery bed.

The above is the method specially employed for lupins and delphiniums. On some others cuttings can be taken from the upper growths of the plant soon after it has finished its first

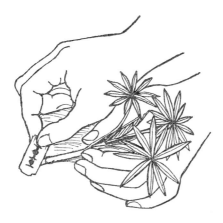

FIG. 3. Making a lupin cutting. Young shoots, about 3–4 ins long are trimmed immediately below a leaf-joint and rooted in a propagating frame

blooming. Examples are pinks, penstemons, anthemis and catmint. You take either 'heel' cuttings or 'nodal' ones.

A heel cutting is a young unflowered side-shoot, 2 or 3 ins long, plucked off from the main stem by a downward tweak. Trim the heel of any loose matter with a very sharp knife, remove all the leaves except the top three or four and plant the cutting in a pot or clay pan, filled with the same compost as mentioned above, which must have been thoroughly moistened. Proceed then as for delphiniums and lupins.

A nodal cutting is of a similar nature, but without the heel of the parent stem. The young side-shoot is cut, with a very sharp knife, immediately below a node, or leaf-joint. Cuttings of both sorts are best taken from the lower parts of the parent plant.

By Root Cuttings

One more method of propagation deserves mention, mainly because it is very important where border phloxes are concerned. This is propagating by root cuttings.

Border phloxes are often attacked by stem eelworm (see

FIG. 4. Root cuttings of herbaceous phlox. The roots are cut up into short pieces and laid in boxes of John Innes Cutting Compost and covered with a thin layer of the same material. New shoots are formed and the young plants are potted on. This is a useful method of increasing border phlox where the stock plants have been attacked by stem eelworm

Chapter VI). If this happens it is useless trying to propagate the plants by division as the divisions will be affected by this pest. Fortunately it does not attack the roots so that plants may be increased quite safely by cutting up their thin, thong-like roots. Each piece of root will produce a new plant quickly.

The job is done between late autumn and early spring and the roots, after they have been dug up, are cut into pieces about 2–3 in long and either laid on their sides in boxes of cutting compost and covered with about $\frac{1}{4}$ in of soil, or dibbled upright into pots of compost. If they are placed upright avoid putting them in upside down. To distinguish between top and bottom cut them across straight at the top and with a slanting cut at the bottom.

Keep the pots or boxes in a frame or cool greenhouse during the winter; new growth should appear in the spring and eventually the new little plants may be set out in their flowering positions or grown on in a nursery bed.

Several other hardy herbaceous perennials may be treated in this way, not because they suffer from stem eelworm but because it is a convenient way of increasing stock. A few roots may be detached for the purpose and the parent plant returned to its position as it will come to no harm if this is done in the dormant season. Such plants include anchusas, hollyhocks, limonium (statice), romneyas, gaillardias, the drumstick primula (*Primula denticulata*), oriental poppies and Japanese anemones.

CHAPTER IV

PERENNIALS AS CUT FLOWERS

M ANY of the popular border plants owe a good deal of their popularity to the fact that they are such excellent cut flowers, lasting well in water. This is no place to discuss flower arrangement as such; it is enough to say that from the garden, especially in summer, it should be possible to cut enough flowers, week after week, to fill the house with lavish displays.

However, continual cutting from the border may lead to a certain amount of family dissension, unless the gardener and the housewife are one and the same person. Even so, it is not everyone who can go on cutting regularly from the border without feeling certain qualms of conscience, knowing that, long-lasting though the blooms may be, they never last quite so long when cut as they will if left on the plant.

The way out of this dilemma is to establish a special cutting bed, the best place for which is the kitchen garden, where sweet peas and other annuals are often grown in rows for cut-flower purposes. Most border plants quickly expand to large clumps which need dividing from time to time, possibly at three- or four-year intervals. One usually finds after dividing them that there are too many pieces to be returned to the border and they are often given away or thrown on the bonfire. It is an easy matter to plant them in the cutting bed, which need have nothing formal about it.

Plants may be established in those odd corners which are found in most gardens, or may be planted in rows. The latter method is possibly the easier as it enables the hoe to be run through to keep down weeds. Some staking will be needed, otherwise some plants will tend to flop and their stems will be anything but straight. But the bed on the whole will need very little attention for some years although the plants will benefit from a certain amount of feeding in the form of a spring mulch and forking over the ground between them in the autumn will be helpful.

In the cutting bed, too, may be planted the surplus seedlings from perennials raised from seed. The bed will also provide replacements for the border and for establishing hardy perennials elsewhere in the garden.

Apart from flowers for immediate use, the cutting bed should provide those which may be dried for use in winter decorations. A good many plants will yield flowers for this purpose and it is always worth experimenting. Some flowers dry very well, keeping much of their colour thoughout the winter. Others lose most of their colour, but oddly enough often gain in attraction as they turn to russets, tans and sometimes to metallic colours which are not at all sombre.

The main thing is to keep the shape of the flower and the stiffness of the stem, which can be done by hanging the stems upside down in small bunches (large bunches are to be avoided as they may be attacked by mildews and moulds). An airy shed or attic, where they can dry slowly, is the best place for the flowers.

Another method, better in a damp summer when the air is humid, is to spread the flowers out, not touching each other, on trays made of wire netting so that the air can circulate round them. Some flowers may have to be cut off from their stems and the flower-head only dried. This may have to be done where the plant has thick, fleshy stems which will not dry easily. The flower-heads are mounted on dried stems obtained from other sources before they are used in arrangements. The cutting bed or the border will usually provide plenty of suitable dried stems of various thicknesses in the autumn or early winter.

Plants that most readily adapt themselves to this treatment are those that naturally like dry soils. They include the cornflower-like catananche, the sea holly (*Eryngium*) with its bristly cones and spiky bracts, the globe thistle (*Echinops*), the sea lavender or statice (now called *Limonium*) and the golden garden yarrows (*Achillea*).

In other plants it is the seed pods that we dry off for their winter effect. Of such are *Iris foetidissima*, which bursts its pods sensationally to reveal the scarlet seeds within, the oriental poppy, the dittany (*Dictamnus*), the 'Chinese lanterns' of *Physalis franchetii* and the fluffy, grey, seed heads of *Senecio tanguticus*.

Flowers, whether they are needed for drying or for immediate use, are best cut when they are dry, in the early evening, rather when the sun is on them or when they are being battered by drying winds. Those which are to be dried usually retain more colour if they are cut soon after they have opened, but here again there is room for experiment by cutting the stems when the flowers are at different stages of development.

A list of plants which provide good cut flowers will be found on page 130. The list is by no means comprehensive; one's own experience is often a better guide than lists such as these, but until experience is gained they give one something on which to base trials and errors.

Anthemis tinctoria

Centaurea macrocephala

Astilbes

Campanula lactiflora

Chrysanthemum maximum 'Esther Read', the most popular Shasta Daisy

Clematis recta, a clematis suitable for the border

Gaillardia aristata

Erigeron macranthus

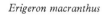

Eryngium planum, a deep blue Sea Holly

Helenium autumnale

Hosta sieboldiana

Hosta crispula

Section of an herbaceous border, delphiniums at the back, heleniums in foreground

CHAPTER V

A CHOICE OF BORDER FLOWERS

THE range of suitable hardy herbaceous perennials for the garden is so wide that there is something to suit every taste. Even a quite small garden might have room for representatives from thirty or forty different genera, while upwards of a couple of hundred might be found in the larger garden. When it is remembered that a comprehensive catalogue may list as many as two hundred genera, some of which may have a score or more of suitable species or anything up to a hundred-named garden varieties (or cultivars), then it will be realised that there is no lack of plant material.

Although it would be impossible in the space allowed to describe more than a fraction of the border plants which might be grown in the small garden, those described below can be guaranteed to give a good account of themselves, provided they are given normal care and attention.

There are many more; some of the better nurseries send out excellent catalogues which provide brief but worth-while descriptions, often with cautionary notes where plants are inclined to ramp or where they have special soil requirements. But, when considering the purchase of any kind of plant, it is always better to see for oneself.

There are plenty of places where herbaceous plants may be seen. Nurseries often welcome visitors (some by appointment only, especially during the busy season); public parks often have well-labelled collections of suitable plants, usually very well grown, as they are in the care of professional gardeners. There are many botanic gardens all over the country where plants may be seen. One normally thinks only of the Royal Botanic Gardens at Kew and Edinburgh, but there are many others, usually attached to the universities, including the so-called 'Redbrick' universities.

In the South there are the famous gardens belonging to the Royal Horticultural Society at Wisley in Surrey. One does not have to be a Fellow of this Society to visit the gardens, for they are open to the general public at a small fee for most of the year except on Sundays.

In the North, at Harlow Car, near Harrogate, there are similar gardens run by the Northern Horticultural Society, in which thousands of plants may be seen.[1] There are fine gardens attached to many National Trust properties and in every county there are numerous private gardens which are open to the public at various times, usually for charitable purposes. Not all of these are large; many of them are quite small and it is in these, perhaps, that the visitor can often gain a better idea of what plants look like in a smaller, more intimate setting. Other valuable sources of information are local and national flower shows (the Royal Horticultural Society hold these fortnightly for most of the year).[2]

It is, of course, perfectly safe to order plants from the nurseryman's catalogue without knowing what they look like. But it is much better to know a little about them first and especially to see them when they are fully established and in full growth and flower. Some, it must be admitted, are over-ex-

[1] A companion volume in this series, *Gardening in the North*, by Mr Kenneth Lemmon, who is honorary secretary of the Society, is full of useful information.

[2] The annual bulletins and occasional news letters and illustrated pamphlets issued by the Hardy Plant Society contain much useful and interesting information. Anyone may join; the annual subscription is only 12s. 6d. The Honorary Secretary is Miss B. White, 10, St. Barnabas Road, Emmer Green, Reading, Berkshire.

uberant in their growth; they are the 'rampers' which must be
employed only after serious consideration, for they may overwhelm their neighbours in the course of a year or two. And
once they have settled into your garden you may find it
difficult to get rid of them or to keep them under control. However, they may still be found a place, provided it is the right
one and I have included a few of them among the plants
described below, with the appropriate warning.

If a plant has a particular soil requirement I have indicated
it. But most of those described will grow on any normal soil.
I have gardened myself on the thinnest of chalky soils, on heavy
intractable clay soils, on poor London soils and on the lightest of
sandy soils, overlying two or three feet of pure sand on a pre-
historic river-bed. I have not gardened on very acid soils, but
generally speaking, these will support most plants, although
the acidity may have to be corrected with generous applications
of lime from time to time.

The more difficult plants have been omitted from this
chapter; there are enough good ones which are undemanding
in their requirements. Those that are fussy in their needs and
demand coddling are either best left to the experts or may be
tried when more experience has been gained.

Acanthus (Bear's Breech). Here we have two excellent
hardy plants in *Acanthus mollis* and *A. spinosus* both of which
grow to about 4 ft tall. They are beautiful in both flower and
leaf, for the large dark-green leaves are deeply cut into long
segments, so ornamental to look at that they have formed the
basis of architectural motifs since the days of the ancient Greeks.
Although they do best on the lighter, sandy soils, they will also
grow well enough on chalky soils and on clay, but on clay
soils good drainage is necessary. In colder areas they need some
protection. They are suitable for the border or for growing in

FIG. 5. The Bear's Breech (*Acanthus spinosus*) is a plant of
architectural appearance with dark green ornamental leaves and
tall spikes of rosy-purple flowers

splendid isolation, where the beauty of their foliage can be appreciated. Both produce tall spikes closely set with large, rosy-purple, hooded flowers in late summer, curiously wrought.

Achillea (Yarrow). An excellent genus this, providing us with plants ranging from less than a foot to 4 ft or so, in several colours, flowering over a long period from midsummer to autumn. Most of them have flat crowns of innumerable small flowers. The dwarf *Achillea clypeolata* has ferny leaves and golden crowns; at about 9 in tall it is quite suitable for the front row of the border. Yellow-flowered also are *A.* 'Moonshine' and *A. taygetea*, the latter primrose-yellow and both about 2 ft tall. The useful cut flower *A. ptarmica* 'Perry's White' also grows to 2 ft. This has button-like heads of white flowers. *A. millefolium*, which has flat heads of cerise flowers, grows a little taller at 3 ft and is a good plant for the centre of the border. There is a good variety of this, 'Fire King', a much brighter red but not quite so tall.

The tallest of the yarrows is the splendid *A. filipendulina* 'Gold Plate' which may grow 5 ft high in good cultivation, needs no staking and has large, golden platters. These turn to the colour of old, dried mustard as they go over, but may be left on the plant to provide extra colour in the garden in autumn. Or the stems may be cut soon after the flowers first open and hung upside down to dry indoors. Then they will retain much of their golden colour for months and are useful for winter vases of dried flowers, always much more interesting and effective than those bowls of plastic flowers which seem to be *de rigueur* in every public house and hotel.

Aconitum (Monkshood). These grow in the manner of the shorter delphiniums and have hooded flowers, like the helmet of Achilles. Here again there is a good range of height, for *Aconitum variegatum bicolor*, with flowers in blue and white, grows only 2 ft tall. Two others, *A. napellus* 'Spark's Variety', with violet-blue flowers, and *A. wilsonii* 'Barker's Variety' with bright blue flowers, are quite suitable for the back of the border or for planting in light woodland as they reach 5 ft. In between these comes the pale-blue *A. fischeri* at 3 ft. All flower in late summer and autumn, thus adding to their value. The roots of monkshoods are highly poisonous to man and beast.

Adonis. There are not a great many spring-flowering herbaceous perennials, so that the keen grower welcomes the few that there are. One of these is *Adonis amurensis flore pleno*, which is in bloom during March and April with the daffodils. It has frond-like leaves and bright yellow double daisy flowers, although it is related to the buttercups not the daisies. It grows about a foot tall and looks splendid when massed.

Ajuga (Bugle). This deserves a place because it is an excellent little ground-cover plant which spreads across the soil, forming a dense mat. It is best employed beneath trees and shrubs, where it will keep down the weeds; less robust plants may be throttled. It may be underplanted with bulbs of various kinds, both spring-flowering and summer-flowering, especially the autumn crocuses which look very attractive when their leafless flowers open above the ground cover of bugle. The best kind is the purple-leaved *Ajuga reptans atropurpurea*. This bears short spikes of blue flowers mainly in spring and early summer.

Alchemilla (Lady's Mantle). *Alchemilla mollis* is another useful ground-cover plant, used with great effect in such delightfully-planted gardens at Hidcote Bartrim Manor, Gloucestershire and Hodnet Hall, Shropshire. It thrives in the partial shade of trees and shrubs and is a fine plant for keeping down weeds. But it is more than this; it is a beautiful foliage plant with large, felted, slightly-lobed leaves. The loose spikes of greenish-yellow flowers are not very colourful but look attractive enough when massed plants are in flower in early summer. In flower it is a foot or so tall. Easy from seed.

Alstroemeria (Peruvian Lily). The *Alstroemeria* 'Ligtu Hybrids' are among the most beautiful of all hardy herbaceous plants, but must also be considered as among the most difficult to establish. In fact one could go so far as to say that it is practically impossible to establish anything but young pot-grown plants. This is because the tuberous roots are as brittle as glass and break even more easily than glass. Sow these seeds in a 4-in pot; they germinate easily. When the seedlings are about 2 in high, knock them carefully out of their pots disturbing the root ball as little as possible.

They are well worth the extra trouble because the flowers, borne in heads on stems 3 ft or so tall, are very beautiful. They look much like those of some azaleas and come in all sorts of colours, including various pinks, creamy-white, buff and flame-red, and are fine for cutting. The older yellow *Alstroemeria aurantiaca* is extremely invasive.

Alyssum. *Alyssum saxatile*, often know as Gold Dust from the bright colour of its myriads of small flowers, is often considered as a rock-garden plant. It is most often seen growing between the bricks or stones of walls, a position for which it is very well suited. But it will also grow on the flat equally well, even in poor soil and is admirable for enlivening the border, or any odd corner, in spring.

As plants age they are inclined to straggle, but this may be overcome to a great extent by trimming them over after they have flowered, without cutting too much into the older growth. This will encourage the formation of many new flowering shoots for the following spring. Apart from the normal golden-flowered kind, there are forms with lemon-yellow flowers (*citrinum*), buff-yellow ('Dudley Neville'), and double golden-yellow (*flore pleno*). All grow about 9 in tall and flower freely from April to June.

Anchusa (Alkanet). Blue-flowered plants suitable for the border are not all that common; the anchusas are among the best of them and are valuable as precursors of the delphinium. The relationship to the humble forget-me-nots is obvious when one looks at the flowers, for each one is like an enlarged version

FIG. 6. The Alkanet (*Anchusa azurea*) is a fine border plant for
early summer with flowers in one shade or another of blue. They
look like giant forget-me-nots

of a forget-me-not. The species offered by nurserymen is *Anchusa azurea* (*italica*) which has a number of garden varieties, including the 5-ft tall 'Morning Glory' which is about the tallest kind and also the kind with the largest flowers, which are a rich bright blue. 'Opal' is not quite so tall; it has sky-blue flowers. Less tall than these are 'Loddon Royalist' with gentian-blue blossoms and 'Pride of Dover', mid-blue.

Flowering usually starts fairly late in May and goes on until July. Plants take up a fair amount of room when fully grown and their corner of the border may look a little colourless when they are over. But this may be overcome to a great extent by ensuring that plants which flower later are grown in front of them. The taller anchusas in particular need adequate staking.

See also under *Brunnera*.

Anemone (Japanese Anemone or Windflower). Most of the anemones are early-flowering rock garden or woodland plants or else tuberous-rooted varieties familiar as cut flowers and treated as half-hardy plants. But the 'Japanese' anemones are fine hardy perennials, particularly valuable because they flower in late summer and autumn and will put up with a good deal of shade.

The form most commonly seen is *Anemone elegans* 'Honorine Joubert' which bears large white flowers, each with a distinctive boss of yellow stamens. There are other forms of *A. elegans* with pink flowers, such as 'Krimhilde' and 'Lorelei' and also a fine semi-double white variety 'Louise Uhink'. Another popular Japanese anemone is the semi-double rose-pink *A. hupehensis japonica*. All these grow about $2\frac{1}{2}$–3 ft tall and their stiff stems need no staking. They do best in a moist soil.

These anemones hate disturbances, must be planted in spring, *not* autumn, and usually sulk the first year. Mark the position of each plant with a label, for they disappear.

Anthemis. Well-grown plants of *Anthemis tinctoria* will provide masses of gay, yellow, daisy-form flowers throughout most of the summer and early autumn. Two good garden varieties are usually available: 'Beauty of Grallagh', deep yellow, and 'E. C. Buxton', an old favourite with sulphur-yellow blooms. All grow about $2\frac{1}{2}$ ft tall and need little staking. Plants will yield a long succession of cut flowers and are increased by stem cuttings or are raised by spring-sown seed. Worth mentioning, too, although it is not quite hardy every where, is *Anthemis cupaniana*, a choice grey-leaved plant which smothers itself with white, golden-centred daisies from June to late September or even October.

Aquilegia (Columbine, Granny Bonnets, etc.). The columbines, with their elegant flowers dancing airily on slender stems are valuable plants for partial shade, flowering from May onwards. The best kinds are those with very long spurs, such as the 'McKana Hybrids' and 'Mrs Scott-Elliott's Strain'. In these the 4-in wide flowers may have curving spurs 3–4 in long. The colour range is wide; it includes soft pinks and yellows, blues, maroons, purples, reds, creams and white.

These are very easily raised from seed sown in spring but, if it is desired to group together several plants of the same colour or approximately the same colour, then the seedlings should be allowed to flower first in the nursery bed and should then be labelled so that when they are moved to their final flowering quarters they may be grouped properly. They grow about $2-2\frac{1}{2}$ ft tall, like a rich soil and grow well in the semi-shade cast by trees.

Arabis. Like the alyssums described on page 55, *Arabis albida flore pleno* is usually seen on rock gardens or growing as a wall plant. But on the rock garden it is inclined to ramp and may overwhelm smaller, more delicate plants. However, in the spring border, associated with alyssums and aubrietas, its vigorous growth can be a decided asset. In any case it should be cut back fairly hard after it has flowered. It covers itself with its double white flowers throughout the spring. At 9 in tall it is suitable for the front of the border.

Armeria (Thrift). Again plants often seen on rock gardens but also suitable for edging borders or for growing in spaces between paving stones on terraces and the like. Thrifts make symmetrical dome-like mounds of grassy leaves from which appear taller stems bearing the flowers which are familiar enough to those who have looked on the back of a 12-sided 3*d*. piece of King George VI's reign. For the border, the best thrifts are *Armeria maritima*, a native plant with pink flowers, making 6 in, its white form *alba* and *A. plantaginea* 'Bee's Ruby' which, at 18 in, is the tallest of these charming and tidy little plants. The latter also flowers later, from June to August, by which time the native plant is over.

Aruncus (Goat's Beard). *Aruncus sylvester* (once called *Spiraea aruncus*) is still often referred to as a spiraea, although the true spiraeas are all shrubs. It is one of the most spectacular of hardy plants when properly grown in deep rich soil and partial shade for then it will produce numerous 4-ft tall plumes of tiny creamy-white flowers during June and early July. It is an easy plant, but is usually better grown as a specimen (or group of specimens where there is room), for then it can be allowed the space it needs to develop properly and can be better appreciated.

Aster (Michaelmas Daisy). One is tempted to wonder some-times what our gardens would look like in the autumn without the Michaelmas daisies. Planting up a border without these valuable plants would be like playing *Hamlet* without the Prince. Most of them are fine as cut flowers, although a few varieties tend to curl their petals in a disagreeable way when they are brought indoors for use in flower arrangements. The choice of varieties is very wide, but I suggest that the following may be worth considering. The *amellus* varieties are charming, with their large bosses of golden stamens contrasting with the petal colour. For garden purposes, there is little difference between the *novae-angliae* and the *novi-belgii* varieties.

TALL (4–5 ft)

A. ericoides 'Ringdove', rosy pink.

A. novae-angliae 'Barr's Pink' and 'Harrington's Pink', two fine old varieties.

A. novi-belgii 'Beechwood Charm' (crimson), 'Beechwood Triumph' (rose-red), 'Climax' (light blue, old, but still fine), 'Eventide' (violet-purple), 'Lassie' (pure pink), 'The Archbishop' (purple-blue) and 'White Ladies'.

MEDIUM (2–4 ft)

A. amellus 'Blue King' (bright blue), 'Mauve Beauty' and 'Ultramarine.'

A. novi-belgii 'Apple Blossom' (blush-pink), 'Beechwood Challenger' (rosy-crimson, another fine old-timer), 'Crimson Brocade' (deep red), 'Gayborder Royal' (rosy-crimson), 'Mistress Quickly' (true blue), 'Orlando' (clear pink, single) and 'Patricia Ballard' (rich pink).

DWARF (to 2 ft)

A. novi-belgii 'Audrey' (lilac-mauve, 12–15 in), 'Court Herald' (rosy-lilac, 12 in), 'Little Red Boy' (rosy-red, 15–18 in), 'Pink Lace' (12–15 in) and 'Snowsprite' (9 in).

The taller asters in particular grow to their tallest and produce their largest flowers when the plants are drastically thinned in the late spring or early summer, cutting out all but a dozen shoots.

It pays to lift the plants every alternate year and split them up into quite small pieces and replant them; they will rapidly increase in girth and one is inevitably landed with many surplus plants. Before giving or throwing these away, reserve sufficient for the cutting bed or for planting in odd places in the garden to provide autumn colour. Most asters may be so split up in the autumn or spring, but it is unsafe to do this at any time except the spring with the *amellus* varieties. In fact, unless the largest flowers are needed for, say, exhibition purposes, the *amellus* varieties need not be divided for several years.

Tall varieties need a fair amount of staking and tying in as they develop otherwise heavy rain and wind will cause them to flop over untidily. The dwarf varieties need little, if any, staking, nor need they be divided frequently. The very dwarf kinds, those growing up to about 15 in tall, look best when they are massed together. Those awkward narrow beds, too narrow for rose bushes, which often flank paths from the house to the gate, may well be filled with them. Admittedly there will be little colour until late summer, although this can be overcome by interplanting with a suitable summer-flowering hardy plant of similar height such as *Inula ensifolia*. Spring colour may be provided by underplanting with bulbs.

Astilbe. These are the plants which some gardeners still call spiraeas, because of their handsome plumes. They are complex hybrids available in a number of named varieties, all delightful plants for rich, deep, moist soils. They do very well in the boggy soils round pools or ponds in the shade cast by surrounding trees or shrubs. They may also be forced in the greenhouse for early flowering but should afterwards be planted out in the open garden. Heights are from about 2 to 5 ft.

The tallest is probably 'Betsy Cuperus', but its white flowers tend to droop more than those of other kinds, which carry their plumes elegantly erect. 'Avalanche', white, 'Bridal Veil', cream, 'Pink Pearl', and 'W. Reeves', dark crimson, are good varieties of medium height, about 3 ft. The popular garnet-red 'Fanal' grows to about 2 ft or a little more and has distinctive reddish leaves.

Even moist soils tend to dry out in periods of drought and the astilbes may suffer from lack of moisture unless the area is thoroughly flooded occasionally with the hose.

Aubrieta. I make no apology for including the aubrietas, normally looked on as rock-garden plants, in a book on hardy herbaceous perennials, for, with the alyssums and arabis described above, they form an indispensable trio for providing spring colour. They will grow well enough on level ground, although, if a bank or slope can be provided for them, where their growths, which are naturally trailing, can hang down, they will be more effective.

There are so many colourful kinds nowadays that one can forget the old, rather dull, purple kinds. The crimsons such as 'Bonfire', 'Crimson Queen', the pinks such as 'Gloriosa', 'Maurice Prichard' and 'Riverslea Pink', and the red 'Mrs Rodewald' are beautiful plants, free-flowering over several weeks. But the violet 'Godstone' and the lavender 'Studland' should not be neglected. Alternatively, aubrietas can be grown from seed with great care, but you take pot-luck for their colour.

Aubrietas become terribly shabby unless they are trimmed over quite hard with a pair of shears or scissors after their flowering has finished. This and a little rich soil worked in among the growths will encourage them to make plenty of new flowering growth.

Balloon Flower. *See Platycodon*

Baptisia. I have never been very successful with *Baptisia australis*, possibly because I have not given it the soil it likes – a well-drained, rather dry one with a place in the full sun. I include it here, however, because of its spikes of delightful dark-blue pea flowers borne amid glaucous-green foliage throughout the early summer. The plant grows about 4 ft or so tall and makes a bush nearly as much through in course of time.

Bergamot. *See Monarda*

Bergenia. The bergenias, still sometimes called megaseas or saxifrages, are among the earliest of hardy plants to come into flower in spring. They are hardly suitable for the border proper, perhaps, and are best suited to informal situations in partial shade. Their large, shining, leathery leaves make them

Fig. 7. One of the reliable plants for spring is the Large-leaved Saxifrage (*Bergenia cordifolia*). Its rosy-pink flowers appear on thick, fleshy stems in March and April

interesting foliage plants when out of flower, especially if care is taken to cut off dead or dying leaves, which otherwise disfigure the clumps. The leaves sometimes turn reddish in winter but this should not be taken as an indication that they are dying. The flowers are carried in large, arching sprays about a foot high.

The species usually seen is *Bergenia cordifolia*, which has rose-pink flowers in March and April. But a number of hybrids has been developed in recent years and it is worth keeping an eye open for them. They grow to a foot or so tall when in flower. Increase by division.

Bleeding Heart. *See Dicentra*

Brunnera. The plant often known as *Anchusa myosotidiflora* is correctly, but less euphoniously, named *Brunnera macrophylla*. Its long, airy sprays of large forget-me-not flowers are welcome in late spring; its leaves, which by summer have become large and coarse, are less welcome. Do not be misled by its spring appearance, when the leaves are still small, into planting it too near other plants in the front of the border, otherwise they will disappear by the time summer is at its height, smothered by the brunnera leaves. Keep it well away from smaller plants or plant it by itself. Despite this warning it is a fine and useful specimen which seems to grow in any soil, heavy clay or thin chalk, provided it has a reasonably sunny place.

Bugle. *See Ajuga*

Campanula (Bellflower). The beautiful campanulas range from the delicate little species grown on the rock garden, sometimes successfully, sometimes not, to the coarse but still handsome Chimney Bellflower (*C. pyramidalis*), usually grown as a biennial but truly a perennial and behaving as such in warmer situations.

One of those grown on the rock garden deserves mention here, for it is an excellent plant for the same sort of uses as

FIG. 8. The clusters of deep purple-blue flowers of *Campanula glomerata* are borne for most of the summer

aubrieta. This is *C. portenschlagiana*, an unfortunate mouthful for the pretty plant which we grew up to know more attractively as *C. muralis*. It quickly makes a big trailing clump a mere 3 or 4 in tall but covering a quite large area with a sheet of purplish blue.

There are several true border bellflowers, all of great value, not only for their intrinsic beauty, but also for their willingness to grow in shady places. The tallest is *C. lactiflora*, which may easily reach 5 ft, thus qualifying for a place towards the back of the border, or for the centre if the border is a 'walk-round' one. It bears numerous sprays of pale blue or mauve-blue flowers during the summer. There is a variety, 'Loddon Anna' which has lilac-pink flowers, distinctly different from the usual blues or whites of the border bellflowers. It does not quite reach the height of the blue kind.

C. latifolia 'Brantwood' at 4 ft is another fine plant, with violet-purple flowers until late summer. But none of these is quite as good as the Peach-leaved Bellflower, *C. persicifolia* and its varieties, which bear large flowers of true bell shape, very like those of the Canterbury Bell. There are various-named varieties all of which grow to about 3 ft tall. 'Beechwood' has pale-blue flowers, 'Fleur de Neige' double white, 'Snowdrift' single white and 'Telham Beauty', the best of all the blues, and one of the prime choices for any garden.

For the front of the border an excellent plant is *C. glomerata dahurica* with dense clusters of very deep purple-blue flowers all the summer, on foot-tall stems. Like all the herbaceous bellflowers, it is happy in shade, even quite dense shade.

All these campanulas are easily increased by division.

Campion. *See Lychnis*

Carnation. *See Dianthus*

Catmint. *See Nepeta*

Catananche (Cupid's Dart). With flowers like large corn-flowers, *Catananche caerulea* is as useful for cutting as the annual cornflowers themselves, even though they are lavender-blue rather than true blue. There is a white form 'Perry's White'; both grow to about 2 ft. Planting should be delayed until the spring and a warm position should be chosen to enable the plants to give of their best. The flowers are some-what chaffy in appearance and in common with other flowers of this kind they may be cut and dried for adding to the bowls of dried flowers for winter decoration.

Centaurea (Knapweed). Don't be put off by the name 'Knapweed'; the centaureas are good garden plants. In par-ticular, *C. macrocephala* usually attracts attention for it grows 4–5 ft tall, a branching plant, bearing large yellow, thistle-like flowers, often 3 in across, in late summer. *C. montana* is like a blue cornflower; it has varieties with red, pink and white flowers. These all grow to about 2 ft and flower from late May onwards.

Cephalaria. The flower of the cephalaria looks just like a yellow scabious. Two are sometimes seen in gardens, *C. alpina* which despite its name grows to 5 ft tall, and *C. tatarica* which grows even taller and in a rich heavy soil has with us exceeded 6 ft. Both are oddly attractive plants although rather spare in appearance with branches held out at 45° angles from dense foliage. In the former species the flowers are a pale sulphur-yellow; in the other they are slightly deeper. Both flower in summer and are best planted at the back of the border where their sparseness of growth may be hidden.

Chrysanthemum. The early-flowering outdoor chrysan-themums are dealt with in another book in this series. Here one should mention one or two hardy plants which require much less attention than the florist's chrysanthemums. The major one is *C. maximum*, the well-known Shasta Daisy, typi-fied for most gardeners by the double white variety 'Esther Read'. Perhaps because it is so well known it has overshadowed other good varieties such as 'Beauté Nivelloise', a much longer-petalled kind, 'Horace Reed', creamy white, 'Everest' a fine single white, and 'Thomas Killin', reminiscent of the anemone-centred florist's chrysanthemums. All these should be planted in spring rather than autumn. They grow 2½–3 ft tall.

These flower in summer and by autumn they are usually over. But then their places are taken by *C. rubellum*, of which 'Clara Curtis' is the best variety, with clear pink flowers on 2½ ft stems. Flowering about the same time is the 5 ft tall Moon Daisy, *C. uliginosum*, a plant which has been neglected in recent years in favour of the Shasta Daisies. But it is still a good late-flowering plant with wide white, yellow-centred single flowers until well on into the autumn, valuable for cutting.

These types of chrysanthemum are readily increased by division.

Cimicifuga (Bugbane). Plants which do well in shade are especially useful for not all of us have open, sunny gardens. In the light shade of trees, especially where the soil is moist, the cimicifugas may be planted. They produce slender spikes of feathery flowers in late summer. There are several species, all in white, differing in height and also in minor details of flower and foliage which need not concern the gardener. *C. americana (cordifolia)*, *C. dahurica* and *C. foetida intermedia* all grow to about 4 ft. This is exceeded by *C. racemosa*, the Snake-root, so called because it was used by North American Indians to cure rattle-snake bites, a use which will find little application in our gardens, just as the old Russian use of certain species for driving away bugs will not, we hope, be needed by gardeners here.

Clematis. The popularity of the climbing clematis has tended to overshadow the several herbaceous species, so that they are not seen very often. One of the best is *C. recta purpurea* because even when it is not producing its sprays of small white fragrant flowers, which it does for most of the summer, it is a handsome plant for it has purple leaves. It makes a mound of thin growths, needing twiggy staking, about 3 ft tall. The green-leaved kind grows a little taller as do both the pale-blue *C. davidiana*, the deep-blue *C. heracleaefolia* 'Côte d'Azure', both

FIG. 9. The Bugbanes (*Cimicifugas*) are excellent plants for growing in the light shade under trees. This is *Cimicifuga foetida intermedia*, a 4-ft tall plant with white flowers in late summer

of which flower in autumn, and *C. integrifolia* which smothers itself with small violet, bell-shaped flowers all through the summer and autumn.

Columbine. *See Aquilegia*

Coreopsis (Tickseed). These popular little daisy-flowered plants should be in every border, as they add much brightness for much of the summer. In height they range from the 18-in tall bright yellow *C. verticillata*, a graceful plant with delicate foliage, almost as slender in habit as that of an asparagus, to the 3 ft or so of *C. grandiflora* and its varieties. Of these 'Baden-gold' has golden flowers. 'Mayfield Giant' is orange-yellow and 'Sunburst', a somewhat shorter variety, is also golden. All these are good for cutting. The other popular species is *C. auriculata superba*, which reaches about 2 ft and is distinctive in that its yellow flowers have crimson-maroon centres. All these coreopsis deserve a sunny place. Increase by division or sow seed in spring.

Cranesbill. *See Geranium*

Curtonus (Aunt Eliza). Until one realises that *Curtonus paniculatus* was once named *Antholyza paniculata* it is difficult to know why it is known as 'Aunt Eliza'. It is very like a giant montbretia, its stiff stems reaching up to 4 ft, with a certain angular grace. The flowers, about twice as large or more as those of monbretias, are orange-scarlet and are borne late in the summer. Although the usual recommendation is a light, sandy soil, I have found that it does well in heavier soils provided they are well drained. It does not mind a little shade.

Cynara (Globe Artichoke). Whether you have cultivated a taste for the undeveloped flower-heads of the globe artichoke or not, it is a handsome plant, although not one for the very small garden. A small group can look most effective against the dark background of a hedge or fence, for the beauty lies in the large bluish-green leaves. In rich, well-manured soil, which the plant needs if it is to be grown in the kitchen garden to provide a crop, it may reach 6 ft. In the border, where the soil is scarcely so rich, it is usually 4–5 ft tall. Plants are set out in spring about 3 ft apart. If the large, rounded, thistle-like flower heads are left on, as they should be in the border, they open a fine blue.

Delphinium. This is perhaps a difficult time to write about the perennial larkspur, for we shall soon see the emergence of exciting new varieties in tones of red, pink and yellow, *and* scented varieties, as the result of brilliant work in Holland by Dr R. L. Legro. He has broken the 'chromosome barrier' to introduce into our garden strains these colours that belong to some wild species with which the average gardener is not familiar.

Meanwhile, there is plenty of choice from among the magnificent blues, mauves and whites to which we have become accustomed. These are hybrids of *D. elatum*. They are now classified into 'tall', 'medium' and 'short' varieties. The shorts, which do not normally exceed 4 ft, are everybody's flower, requiring staking in only very exposed places. Out of a growing class, Blue Tit, Blue Jade and Betty Bazely are splendid exemplars.

The taller sorts, which queen it over all the flowers of the border at high summer, *must* be staked, but 4-ft canes are quite long enough, four to a full-grown plant. There is an embarrassing choice before one, but it may help to note that the top five in the Delphinium Society's analysis in 1963 were Silver Moon, Daily Express, Mogul, Swan Lake and Purple Triumph.

Culture. Delphiniums need good cultivation, with well-dug soil and plenty of manure or a substitute. Their only serious enemy is the slug, from which they can be protected by scraping away the top inch of soil and covering the crowns with sharp horticultural sand.

The secret of producing fine spikes is to limit their number – one in the first year, two or three in the second and up to five subsequently. Cut the excess shoots down to the ground before they are 6 in high. After flowering, you may either cut the stems down to the ground, when you will get a second flowering, or cut off the flower spike only, which is better for the future vigour of the plant.

All delphiniums come fairly easily from seed, sown in spring, but they will be a mixed bag. The Pacific Giants are selected in colour groups and are quick and easy. Named varieties can be reproduced only by cuttings, as described in Chapter III.

A totally different class of delphinium is the 'belladonna'. This does not have dense spikes, but carries its spurred florets loosely to about 3 ft; there are several varieties, all easy.

Dianthus (Border Carnations and Pinks). Like Johnny Walker, 'Mrs Sinkins' is still going strong, but she bursts her calyx shamelessly and there are now much better scented white pinks in 'Lillian' (an Allwoodii pink) and 'Whiteladies'.

There are innumerable strains and named varieties of border carnations and pinks. Of the smaller pinks, try the single red, crimson-centred 'Betty Norton' the double-flowered 'Dad's Favourite', white splashed with chocolate, the double pale-pink 'Inchmery' and the dark-red double 'Thomas'. All these grow about 8–9 in tall and like a sunny place in front of the border.

The same situation suits the somewhat taller Border Pinks in which the colour range is wider and includes such delightful shades as French grey found in 'Harmony', in which the petals are striped with cerise; and apricot-pink as in 'Desert Song', flushed with greyish lavender. Yellow is found in 'Ettrickdale', white in 'White Ensign' and crimson in 'Oakfield Clove'.

There are many other pink and red varieties, as well as the 'Allwoodii' dianthus, which are hybrids between carnations and pinks, growing about 18 in tall in many colours, as well as Laced Pinks in which the petals are edged with another colour.

All these dianthus benefit from the addition of lime or mortar rubble to the soil, except on chalky soils. But they do not need too rich a soil. Well-grown plants are attractive even when not in flower for they make rounded cushions of grassy, grey-green leaves.

All these pinks are readily increased by young unflowered side-shoots.

Dicentra (Bleeding Heart, Lucy Locket, etc). *Dicentra spectabilis*, once established, needs little attention apart from a mulch in early spring. It may be left in the same position for years and will produce its attractive heart-shaped flowers on arching stems unfailingly each spring. These are rosy-red and white, the white coming from the inside petals, which protrude beyond the outer as the flowers open. Plants may reach 2 ft tall but are usually less than this. They may be forced in the greenhouse for early flowering in pots. *D. eximea* is similar but only 1 ft tall and bears rosy-red flowers for most of the summer. Both have handsome ferny foliage and flourish in semi-shade. Look out for slugs, which are specially fond of bleeding hearts.

Day Lily. See *Hemerocallis*

Dictamnus (Dittany). Apart from the fact that it is one of those plants with a 'parlour trick', *Dictamnus albus* is a fine hardy plant, flowering during June and July. It grows about 2 ft, producing its white flowers in spikes, the petals spreading with long, curved, protruding stamens. A more colourful variety is the rosy-red *purpureus*. The names Burning Bush or Gas Plant refer to the fact that the upper parts of the stems have oil-bearing glands, which in hot weather give off a volatile gas that may be ignited by holding a lighted match near the stem. The result is a momentary flash which is seen better against a dark background. The plant is not harmed.

Digitalis (Foxglove). Most of the foxgloves are biennials and thus do not come within the scope of this book. But there are hardy perennials, of which one at least is a showy plant worth its place in any border. This is the hybrid *D. mertonensis*, produced by the John Innes Institute, which has most attractive flowers of the colour usually described accurately as

FIG. 10. Spring sees the rosy-red and white heart-shaped
flowers of the Bleeding Heart (*Dicentra spectabilis*), a charming
'old fashioned' plant with ferny foliage

crushed stawberry. It grows 2 ft tall. One of its parents is *D. ambigua*, a 3-ft tall perennial plant with pale-yellow flowers for most of the summer. Easily raised from seed.

Dimorphotheca (Cape Marigold). For long considered a half-hardy plant, *D. barberiae* must now be rated as hardy, at least in the southern part of the country, for it regularly survives a good many degrees of frost and with us has not been killed by temperatures of 12-15° F., when protected by a snow covering, although it has certainly been damaged. Since it makes extensive clumps, its spreading stems often rooting into the ground where they touch, it is worth detaching a few of these and growing them on in the cold frame during the winter as a precautionary measure. The plant bears rosy-lilac daisy flowers 2 in or so across. Although the main flowering period is summer, there is scarcely a month when a flower cannot be found, even in the depths of winter. All it needs is a sunny place and well-drained soil, and it isn't really fussy about the latter requirement, as we have grown it very well on heavy Kent clay. The slender stems may be carried a foot or so above the plant.

There is a dwarfer form, less sprawling in habit, known as *compacta*, said to be hardier, but we have never grown this one.

Dodecatheon (Shooting Stars). Given a moist soil and some shade, *Dodecatheon meadia* is not difficult to grow. It does well by the sides of streams or under trees, provided the soil is well drained. It is an attractive plant, a foot or so tall, which in late spring and early summer bears pink-and-white or lilac-and-white flowers faintly resembling those of cyclamen, with much reflexed petals and protruding stamens.

Doronicum (Leopard's Bane). The earliest of the daisies to flower, the doronicums are valuable border plants for their bright colour from March to June. All have golden-yellow flowers varying slightly in the depth of yellow and height of stem. The earliest to flower is *D. austriacum*, a 2-ft tall plant.

D. plantagineum excelsum, otherwise known as 'Harpur Crewe', flowers from April to June and grows to about 3 ft tall.

Plants are best grown in groups for effect, or in the cutting bed for early cut flowers. They do well below deciduous trees, as they flower before the leaf-canopy thickens. An odd point about them is that they may be moved while they are in bud or even when the flowers have opened and, provided they are kept moist for a few days, they will recover quickly. They do very well on chalky soils. Easily increased by division.

Echinacea (Purple Cone Flower). This is another popular, late summer, daisy-flowered plant closely related to the rud-beckias. The species grown here is *Echinacea purpurea*, a 3-ft tall plant bearing large daisies with broad, somewhat reflexed petals and a prominent button-like dark centre. The petal colour varies from a rosy-pink with a hint of blue to purplish-crimson.

A better plant and one which is seen more often, is the selected form 'The King', which, when well grown, may top 5 ft easily and will have rich crimson flowers 5 in across. It is an easy plant needing only a sunny place and a well-drained soil.

Echinops (Globe Thistle). Few plants have such symmetrically-globular flower-heads as the globe thistles, fine plants for the centre or back of the border, flowering in summer and making bold, handsome masses when established. Once again they are not difficult, needing only a well-drained soil and sunny position. The tallest is probably *E. sphaeroce-phalus*, which may reach 6 ft. But it is not quite so colourful as some others, as its flower-heads are silvery whereas in the better kinds they are blue; bright blue in *E. humilis* 'Taplow Blue', deeper in *E. ritro*, both plants about 4–5 ft tall. There is also white form, *nivalis*, of *E. humilis*, which shows up well against darker backgrounds.

Eremurus (Fox-tail Lily or Giant Asphodel). These

handsome plants send up tall, erect, tapering spikes, clothed with small, saucer-shaped florets. Although their season is a short one they are most impressive plants while they are there. Possibly the stateliest of garden plants, they need a rich, light soil and a position where they can be protected from wind in summer, together with some protection for the crowns in winter, which should be removed in spring as the fat growth-buds appear.

The really tall species such as the pink-flowered *E. elwesii* and *E. robustus* are too tall for the small garden as they may soar to 10 ft. It is better to plant the 5-ft yellow-flowered *E. bungei*, or, better still, the modern 'Shelford Hybrids', which are about 6 ft tall and have flowers in pink, yellow, copper, apricot, etc. They look best when grouped.

The fleshy roots are very brittle and must be handled carefully. They are planted in the autumn with the crown about 3 in below the surface and thereafter they should remain undisturbed. They are likely to sulk the first year. After flowering in May and June, the stems should be cut down; the long narrow leaves then turn colour and die down and by July they may be pulled off. Mark the positions of the plants in some way, to avoid damaging the crowns when the border is tidied up in the autumn.

Erigeron (Fleabane). For a good many years the most popular erigeron was *E. macranthus*, earlier known as *E. mesagrandis*, a 2-ft tall plant having violet-daisy flowers with numerous slender ray-florets. This is still a good plant, although it is inclined to flop if not staked, but the last decade has seen the introduction of a number of delightful hybrids, with such characteristic names as 'Charity', light pink, 'Serenity', large-flowered, deep mauve, 'Sincerity', bluish-mauve with yellow centre, 'Prosperity', deep blue, and 'Unity' and 'Vanity', both pink.

All these grow about 2 ft or so tall and are excellent for cutting. They are undemanding in their requirements, needing only a sunny place, although it pays to cut their stems down after they have finished flowering.

Worth mentioning, too, is the pretty little daisy-like *E. mucronatus*, only about 9 in tall and a useful plant for the cracks between paving stones. It is easily raised from seed and flowers with informal abandon all summer.

Eryngium (Sea Holly). The sea hollies are known by their bristly, teazel-like flower cones, encircled by spiky bracts of metallic hue and arising from rather spiny foliage. The most familiar is *E. oliverianum*, 3–4 ft tall, with amethyst-blue flowers. Another popular kind is the deep-blue *E. planum*, 2 ft in height. Both have much-branched stems. There are one or two others of this kind, all summer-flowering, all hardy. They are among the best flowers to dry off for winter.

Once one strays out of the normal run of these eryngiums, it is possible to find several others, which, although they may not be quite bone-hardy everywhere, will survive in gardens in the southern half of the country. We have, for instance, grown successfully in an exposed garden in Kent, *E. bromeliifolium* which survived a dozen or more degrees of frost and thus might be classed as 'reasonably hardy'. It makes a fine foliage plant, a symmetrical clump of narrow, saw-tooth edged leaves, well over 4 ft long. It did not flower every year with us, but when it did it was spectacular with a flower stem 7 or 8 ft high, bearing small heads of white flowers, turning brown as they aged.

Euphorbia (Spurge). The herbaceous spurges are most attractive plants characterized not by their flowers, which are inconspicuous, but by the coloured bracts which surround them and which keep their colour for months. One, in particular, *Euphorbia epithymoides* (*polychroma*), might even qualify as a spring-bedding plant, a purpose for which I have seen it used in the Keukenhof in Holland. For weeks it is a foot-tall mound of golden-yellow. It is evergreen, or practically so, whereas the stems of *E. sikkimensis* die off, as do those of most herbaceous perennials, and are cut down in the autumn.

There is a long season of interest with *E. sikkimensis* from the time the young leaves appear, brilliant red, in the spring, through summer when the golden flower bracts are much in evidence, to autumn when the leaves colour as well as those of many trees and shrubs grown for their autumn colour. They grow about 3 ft or so high and spread to make clumps of good size quite rapidly.

Another hardy herbaceous spurge is the more usual *E. wulfenii*, a 4-ft tall plant, a good deal more sombre in appearance than the other two, but an evergreen, more useful as a specimen plant or group of specimens, than in the border, perhaps. Its stout stems are well-clothed with narrow bluish-green leaves. The flower-bracts here are greenish-yellow and a well-grown plant is a pleasant sight. It does best in a light, well-drained soil.

Evening Primrose. *See Oenothera*

Filipendula (Meadow Sweet). These decorative plants, with waving plumes or crests, were formerly known as spiraeas, which gives an indication of their appearance. They are for moist borders where the soil is rich and deep. They like sun so where the soil dries out quickly plenty of organic material should be dug in and the surface mulched deeply to conserve moisture. *F. rubra magnifica*, the Queen of the Prairie, is the largest and one of the most decorative as when in full flower it is 6 ft tall with beautiful sprays of small, mid-pink flowers in late summer and early autumn. *F. ulmaria flore pleno* is the double form of our native meadow sweet, with creamy-white flowers, and *F. camtschatica rosea*, which needs even more moisture than the others, has very large leaves and clouds of pink flower in late summer. In *F. purpurea* the flower-heads are flatter and crimson in colour.

Flax. *See Linum*
Foxglove. *See Digitalis*
Foxtail Lily. *See Eremurus*

Gaillardia. I assume that the colloquial American name 'Blanket Flower' refers to the way in which a patch of these flowers resembles the highly-coloured blankets produced by the Navajo Indians of Arizona, where some species are found in the wild. Certainly they are among the most colourful of all border plants and first-class bargains, for they flower from June to October and last well when cut. *G. aristata grandiflora* is available as a mixed strain with broadly-petalled flowers richly marked in various ways, yellows, oranges, bronzes and wine-reds predominating. There are named varieties which are more useful when a particular colour scheme is planned. These include the deep red 'Burgundy', the deep yellow 'Golden Queen', the orange-red 'Wirral Flame' and the bronze-yellow 'Torchlight'. All grow 2–3 ft tall and are best planted in spring rather than autumn.

Galega (Goat's Rue). Good tempered pea-flowered plants which need no staking and which can be left happily to their own devices appeal to many gardeners. Among such plants is *Galega officinalis* in its several forms. It is a much easier plant than the other pea-flowered plant, *Baptisia australis*, mentioned earlier. Its one fault, perhaps, is that it will spread beyond its allotted space unless checked. Pieces chopped out of the clumps in the border to keep them within bounds should be planted in the cutting bed, for this is a fine cut flower, distinctly and pleasantly fragrant. The normal colour is bluish-mauve and plants grow about 4–5 ft high. But there is a charming white variety, *alba*, a mauve and white variety, 'Duchess of Bedford', about 3 ft tall, and a pinkish-mauve kind, 'Lady Wilson', only a little taller.

Gentiana. The dwarf gentians seen on the rock garden are not for discussion in this book. But *G. septemfida*, dark blue, beautiful and easy, is very suitable for the front of the border, making a nearly prostrate mat a foot wide. The Willow Gentian, *G. asclepiadea*, a graceful plant some 2 ft tall, with willow-like leaves and arching stems bearing blue trumpet flowers, is seen to best advantage in semi-woodland surroundings. Where really moist, boggy conditions can be provided, it is worth growing the Yellow Gentian, *G. lutea*, a somewhat neglected plant, probably because it looks so much coarser than the alpine gentians. This sends up 4 ft tall leafy stems bearing yellow flowers.

Geranium (Cranesbill). I feel that the hardy geraniums suffer from the confusion in nomenclature, for the name 'geranium' is so firmly entrenched for the tender pelargoniums used for summer bedding. Unsuspecting new gardeners are usually surprised when they are told that the large patch of cranesbill growing in the border is a geranium. The plants deserve to be better known.

By far the best is *G. endressii* of which the best form is 'A. T. Johnson'. In full sun this may reach 18 in and from mid June it smothers itself with silvery pink flowers. From then until October there is a continuous display of flowers, particularly if the dead flower-heads of the early flush are cut off. They develop quickly into closely-knit mats of prostrate stems and it is a very easy matter to chop off pieces 3 or 4 in across from round the parent clump to start new plants elsewhere. This may be done in autumn or spring. The plant does equally well in shade, making excellent ground-cover.

In *G. grandiflorum*, 9–12 in tall, the large flowers are blue and produced throughout June and July. *G. psilostemon* is about the most colourful of all these cranesbills for its large magenta flowers have black centres. This grows about 2½ ft tall, flowering during May and June. There are several others, but these are about the best.

Geum (Avens). I have somewhat mixed feelings about geums, probably because I am not enamoured of orange flowers and there seem to be too many orange and tangerine geums about. However, there is no room for personal prejudice in a book such as this and I must say that geums are easy, free-flowering plants worth their place if care is taken to stake them properly to prevent them from straggling. Orange kinds are 'Orangeman' and 'Prince of Orange'. 'Redwings' has more scarlet in the flowers but may still be classed as orange. I prefer the old 'Lady Stratheden' with golden-yellow double flowers and the crimson 'Mrs Bradshaw'. All grow about 2 ft tall.

Globe Artichoke. *See Cynara*

Globe Thistle. *See Echinops*

Goat's Beard. *See Aruncus*

Gypsophila. Favourites for flower arrangers, *Gypsophila paniculata*, single, and its double form 'Bristol Fairy', make clouds of white 3–4 ft tall in summer. They grow well on dryish banks, do exceptionally well on chalk and benefit from the addition of lime or mortar rubble on other soils. They are usually seen in the border or cutting bed but may also be used to clothe dry banks effectively. The pink 'Flamingo', somewhat less tall, makes a change from white and another pink kind 'Rosy Veil' is well suited to front positions in the border for it does not much exceed a foot in height.

Helenium. The daisy-flowered plants may well be said to form the backbone of the border. So many of them are excellent cut flowers, flower over a long period and are undemanding in their requirements. These attributes apply to the heleniums, flowering through late summer and autumn, colourful plants, of which a number of new varieties have been introduced in recent years. Despite my dislike of orange I find the varieties of this colour less difficult to associate with other plants. Some of them, indeed, are orange-bronze or tawny-orange, such as 'Goldfox'. One of the best of all is 'Moerheim Beauty', a fine rich crimson. 'Bruno' is a mahogany-red variety, flowering later than most; the lemon-yellow 'Riverton Beauty' by contrast is often in flower in July. 'Wyndley', bronze-yellow, comes into flower in August, and at 4 ft is one of the taller varieties although it is exceeded in height by 'Chipperfield

Orange' which may reach 5 ft when well grown. Otherwise heights in general are about 3–3½ ft. Easily increased by division in the same way as Michaelmas daisies.

Helianthus (Perennial Sunflower). Some plants need curbing firmly to keep them in their place and this applies in general to the perennial sunflowers. Granted this, they are useful plants for the back of any border or for the roughish places in the garden where their spreading propensities matter less.

Probably the best is the 6-ft tall *H. salicifolius*, for it is less coarse of leaf than others and has charming lemon-yellow daisies borne in large clusters. The largest flowers are borne by the 6 ft tall *H. decapetalus maximus*; they may be nearly 6 in across, single, of typical sunflower shape. The double, golden-yellow, *H. multiflorus* 'Loddon Gold' is another 6-ft tall plant, a variety over 40 years old, but still good. The tallest is *H. sparsifolius* 'Monarch', which may go over 7 ft, is apt to dwarf most other plants and is a spreader.

All these flower from August to October and cut surprisingly well provided the stems are not too long. They seem to be indifferent about soil and do very well in the poorer kinds as their growth is more limited.

Heliopsis. Another sunflower type, but not so tall, less coarse in foliage and less likely to spread than the helianthus. The 4-ft tall 'Golden Sun' has rich golden flowers, the taller *H. gigantea* has bright yellow flowers, semi-double in form, and the excellent variety, 'Light of Loddon', a very free-flowering plant, 4 ft or so in height, is a good bright yellow. All suffer in drought, their leaves dropping disconsolately, but they recover after a good watering.

Helleborus (Hellebores). Most gardeners must be familiar with the Christmas Rose (*Helleborus niger*), which is the earliest hardy plant to come into flower as far as this book is concerned. It is quite possible to have it in flower at Christmas-time provided the clumps are protected with cloches, which not only forces them slightly but also keeps their beautiful white

FIG. 11. The Lenten Rose (*Helleborus orientalis*) starts to flower in January in a mild winter and goes on flowering until March. This is a good plant for a shady corner

flowers free from mud splashes. Floated, almost stemless, in shallow water they are among the most delightful of all cut flowers.

Not long after they finish flowering the first blooms of the Lenten Rose appear. This is *H. orientalis*, a plant very variable in flower colour, but every variation delightful. Purple, crimson and white are the main colours, but this conveys little, for the flowers are variously spotted with purple or crimson. They flower freely and although it is usually recommended that they should not be disturbed, as they may fail to flower for a year or two, we have moved ours to three gardens and they have flowered unfailingly.

The secret is, I think to ensure that the black, fleshy roots are surrounded by plenty of soil. Again, a shady position is usually recommended, but we have found that they do perfectly well in a sunny place, although if you are looking for an early-flowering plant for shade I would unhesitatingly recommend this one. It grows about $1\frac{1}{2}$ ft tall and has large, leathery, evergreen leaves, quite handsome in themselves.

Hemerocallis (Day Lily). The old-fashioned day-lilies, *Hemerocallis flava*, with clear yellow flowers and *H. fulva*, with coppery flowers, are still good plants, not to be despised. They grow well in both dry and moist soils, making very large clumps in the latter, and they do not mind a little shade. Although the trumpet flowers last for a mere day, they are produced in long succession over many weeks from June to August.

But in recent years many fine differently-coloured hybrids have been introduced, mainly from America, and the introduction of new varieties still goes on, these being expensive. The new colours are delightful; they include maroon, found in 'Royalty', 'Black Prince' and 'Bess Vestal'; bronze in 'Imperator'; red in 'Fantasia' and purple in 'Old Vintage'. Many of the varieties have distinctive yellow or golden-yellow throats. Established clumps seldom need disturbing unless it is

FIG. 12. The individual flowers of the Day-lily (Hemerocallis) are fleeting but they are borne in long succession during the summer months

for propagation purposes. A spring mulch of rotted organic material is helpful. The height range is 2–3 ft.

Increase by division (tough) or raise from seed.

Hesperis (Sweet Rocket, Dame's Rocket, Dame's Violet). Many of our older garden plants have been given various names over the centuries and *Hesperis matronalis*, an old 'cottage-garden' plant is no exception. It still retains its popularity because it is deliciously fragrant, particularly in the evening. It grows about 2–3 ft tall and bears white flowers, reminiscent of those of phloxes, during May and June. There is a dwarf white form, *candidissima*, no more than about 15 in tall, and a purple form *purpurea*. Years ago there were double-flowered forms but as these had to be propagated vegetatively they seem to have disappeared from cultivation. Any double forms which turn up in a batch of seedlings ought to be carefully preserved. Plants are easy to grow in rich, moist soil, and they do not mind partial shade.

Heuchera. *Heuchera sanguinea* is the familiar Coral Bells, a plant with attractive rounded leaves and elegant stems 12–18 in tall, bearing small red flowers in airy plumes, much like those of London Pride. Better still are the taller 'Bressingham Hybrids'. These may reach 2 ft and their enlarged plumes come in all shades of red and pink. There are also named varieties of *H. sanguinea*, including the bright red 'Pluie de Feu' and the crimson-scarlet 'Red Spangles'. Worth noting, too, is the hybrid between *Heuchera brizoides* and *Tiarella cordifolia*, known as *Heucherella tiarelloides*, an even more useful edging plant, as it grows in tufts and its flower stems, bearing reddish-pink clouds, are only a foot tall. All these do best on the lighter soils, but are not really fussy and we have grown them well enough on clay.

Hosta (Plantain Lily). In the same way as a Member of Parliament must declare an interest when certain subjects come up for discussion, perhaps I ought to say that the hostas (once known as funkias) are among my favourite foliage plants.

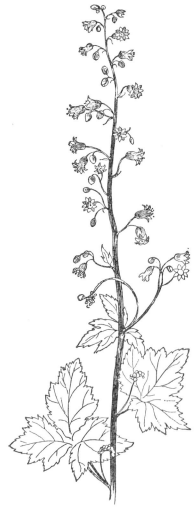

FIG. 13. There is no common name for *Heucherella tiarelloides*,
a delightful edging plant, but one of its parents is *Heuchera
brizoides*, related to the familiar Coral Bells. This hybrid has
reddish-pink flowers on stems a foot tall

Having said that I make no more apology for describing them in glowing terms. They are superb plants for moist shade; they *will* grow in sunny situations, but I have never seen them grow so well there.

One of the finest of all is *H. glauca* (*sieboldiana*) which has large bluish-green leaves and which, when well-suited, will make a clump several feet across and about 2 ft or so tall. It has interesting flowers, but is not grown so much for these as for its foliage; they are pale lilac and open in June.

A little more colourful, though not quite so tall, is *H. undulata*, in which the smaller leaves are variegated with cream in the centre. The flowers are similar but are produced later. In *H. fortunei albo-picta* the leaves have yellowish central variegations.

There are others and it is worth exploring the possibilities of this interesting genus, especially in gardens where there is a fair amount of shade cast by trees and shrubs. To get the best effect the plants need a regular spring mulch with well-rotted compost or manure if it is available. Increase by division (tough).

Incarvillea. This stands alone as a most unusual herbaceous plant, but by no means always an easy one. Once it has been grown the gardener will look forward each year in late spring and summer to seeing once more its large rose-pink trumpets appear on their 2–2½ ft tall stems. Its name, *Incarvillea delavayi*, commemorates two French missionaries who combined the cure of souls with plant hunting in China in the last century. It must have full sun and a light, warm soil that drains really well, to save its fleshy roots from winter rot. It must be planted immediately upon receipt, with its nose just below the surface. Mark the positions of the plants carefully as the leaves die down well before the autumn and it is all too easy to spear the fleshy roots when forking over the border at the end of the season, unless one knows where the plants are.

Iris. This is a vast genus and it is no wonder that in time many gardeners specialise in growing irises in great variety, even though the season is not a long one. Most gardeners will be content with a representative selection of the German or Flag irises, otherwise known as tall bearded irises, flowering in May and June, stately, beautiful plants, well named when one remembers that the Greek goddess Iris was the personification of the rainbow. The choice of varieties is bewildering and a good iris catalogue, issued by such specialist nurseries as Kelway & Son Ltd, of Langport, Somerset, or The Orpington Nurseries Co. Ltd, Orpington, Kent, will list hundreds of varieties and will give reliable colour descriptions.

New varieties are constantly being introduced and are not cheap; of the older ones I can recommend the deep yellow 'Berkeley Gold', the mahogany-red 'Cheerio', a bicolor variety, 'Elmohr' and attractive mulberry-red, 'Loomis V20', an oddly-named but popular kind with shell-pink flowers and a tangerine beard. The same tangerine beard appears in other fine varieties such as the golden-apricot 'Hi Time', the pure pink 'Cameo', the orchid pink 'Radiation' and the canary-yellow 'St. Crispin'.

There are several very dark, almost black varieties which are extremely attractive and not in the least sombre in appearance. They include 'Black Banner', 'Black Forest' in which the dark colour is accentuated by the blue beard, and 'Maisie Lowe'. Blues are found in wide variety and there are many which have red falls or standards (see Fig. 14). The height range is 2–4 ft.

These flag irises appreciate a fair amount of lime or mortar rubble in soils which are not naturally chalky. They must have a sunny position and when their fleshy *stems*, known as rhizomes, are planted, they should lie flat on the ground, with only the roots buried, on either side of the rhizome. The rhizome likes to get a nice baking from direct sun, and this it may fail to get in a leafy border. The enthusiast accordingly grows his irises in special beds of their own.

Established plants make a tangled mass of rhizomes and these

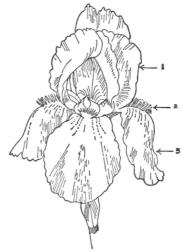

FIG. 14. The flower of a bearded iris. (1) Standards, (2) beard, (3) falls. The various parts are often of different colours

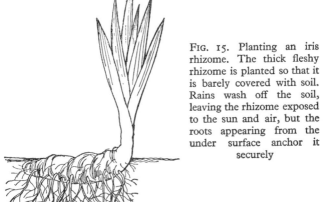

FIG. 15. Planting an iris rhizome. The thick fleshy rhizome is planted so that it is barely covered with soil. Rains wash off the soil, leaving the rhizome exposed to the sun and air, but the roots appearing from the under surface anchor it securely

should be lifted, divided and replanted every fourth year, otherwise their flowering will deteriorate. This is best done immediately after the plants have flowered. Discard the oldest portions and retain only sound, outside pieces which must each have a fan of leaves and some roots. Cut the leaves down to about 6 in, to allow the rhizome to seat itself firmly. A rich soil is not necessary; any ordinary soil will do provided it is reasonably well drained.

Apart from these flag irises, there are the moisture-loving kinds, such as the superb *I. kaempferi*, sometimes known as the 'Orchid Iris', a plant 2 ft or so tall, available in named varieties in a wide range of colours in the blue-purple range, as well as white. This is difficult to grow in this country, needing a wet soil in summer and a dry one in winter. Actually in the boggy soil by the water one may grow *I. laevigata*, with blue or white flowers. Another useful iris for moist soil (or in any that is not too dry) is *I. sibirica*, a fine border plant, with smaller flowers in various shades of blue, purple, violet, etc.

One that should not be neglected is the native Gladdon or Gladwyn iris, *I. foetidissima*, not grown so much for the sake of its slate-grey flowers but for its large seed-heads which split open in autumn to reveal rows of sealing-wax red berries. The stems should be cut as soon as the seed-heads split and before they are damaged by weather and slugs, and used to add brilliant colour to indoor decorations. They will last without falling until the following spring when they gradually shrivel. Sown then, they will germinate quickly if new plants are needed.

Finally, for a dry, sunny place at the foot of a wall, where the soil is poor and stony, there is the winter-flowering *I. unguicularis* (*stylosa*) from which stems of deliciously fragrant lavender-blue flowers may be cut in the early weeks of the year. A rich soil should be avoided, otherwise the plants will produce too much foliage and the flowers will be hidden.

The bulbous irises do not come within my brief.

Kniphofia (Red Hot Poker). These plants are among the most handsome in the border, mainly in late summer, although the red hot poker season actually starts earlier with *K. caulescens*, a 4-ft tall plant which bears buff to red flowers in June. Most of these plants have flowers in one shade or another of red or orange, sometimes combined with yellow, and one of the most spectacular is *K. uvaria*, the common kind with 4-ft tall spikes of scarlet and yellow flowers. There are several others, including the even taller 'Mount Etna', with red to scarlet flowers, and the golden-flowered 'Royal Standard', which is about 3½ ft high. But the most aristocratic looking of all, in my opinion, is 'Maid of Orleans' in which the 4-ft spikes are clothed with ivory-white flowers.

To do these plants well they should be planted in a rich but well-drained soil and fed regularly during the growing season. They need copious watering in dry weather and in colder gardens the evergreen leaves should be tied up over the crown to protect it from frost, during the winter months.

Lathyrus (Everlasting Pea). I have dealt with few climbing plants in this book, mainly because there are so few which might be classified as border plants. But the old-fashioned everlasting pea comes into this category and makes a fine show if given some good support such as stout twiggy sticks up which it can clamber. It will not get out of hand, as it grows only to about 6 ft. The usual colour is rose-red, but equally beautiful are the varieties 'White Pearl' and 'Pink Pearl', both of which come true from seed. Cultivation is easy as the plants are not at all fussy about soil. They may be cut down close to the ground in the autumn in the same way as other herbaceous plants.

Leopard's Bane. See *Doronicum*

Liatris. Few gardeners looking at these plants would connect them with the daisy family for their flowers look very unlike those of any of the cultivated daisies. They are carried in tall, truncheon-like spikes and, what is, perhaps, even more unusual, they open from the top downwards, instead of the other way about. But, all in all, despite their non-conformity, they are fine border plants, flowering over a long period during the summer. A good cluster can look quite spectacular; they are not at all fussy, needing only a sunny position and a reasonably rich light soil. The two species are *L. pycnostachya*, a 4-ft plant with bright purplish-crimson flowers, and *L. spicata* with tightly-packed spikes of purple flowers.

Ligularia. This is the name now given to some of the herbaceous plants (but not to the shrubs) that we used to call senecios. They are bold if rather coarse-leaved plants, often grown in the larger borders but just as suitable for the wilder parts of the garden, especially where the soil is moist, and the plants can get a certain amount of shade. The kind usually seen is *L. clivorum*, a 4-ft tall plant with very large leaves and orange, daisy-form flowers in broad heads.

There are several others which the keen gardener might try, including the variety of *L. clivorum* called 'Othello' which is much the same in flower but has purple-tinted leaves. This purple tint is found also in *L. przewalskii*, which despite its all but unpronounceable name, is a fine plant, about 4 ft tall, in which the leaves are elegantly cut. The tallest of these ligularias are *L. veitchiana* and *L. wilsoniana*, both of which may reach 6 ft and have tall spikes of yellow flowers.

If these are too big there are 3-ft tall varieties of *L. clivorum*, 'Gregynog Gold' and 'Orange Queen'.

Limonium (Sea Lavender). The best of the perennial sea lavenders is the ordinary kind, *L. latifolium*, still known to many gardeners and nurserymen as 'Statice'. This is deservedly popular because the broad spikes of lavender flowers dry so well for winter decoration. It grows to about $2\frac{1}{2}$ ft and is not a fussy plant, although it does better on light soils than on heavy. It should be given a sunny place and if spikes are needed for cutting they should be taken just after they are fully open and when they are dry, not when they are wet with morning dew. Hang them upside down in bunches to dry, in an airy shed or attic.

Linaria (Purple Toadflax). This is not a spectacular plant but it is one of my favourites, mainly because it flowers over such a long period, from late June to September or even into October, and because it is entirely trouble-free, needing no staking and little other attention.

The height normally given is 2 to 3 ft. But don't be misled by this; much depends on situation and soil. The plant seeds itself freely and seedlings which find themselves in poor soils, perhaps in gravel paths or between the bricks of pathways, may grow to less than a foot but will make sturdy, flowerful plants.

On the other hand, plants growing in a reasonably rich soil, without any attention in the way of feeding, will just about reach 4 ft. They make handsome specimens, often nearly a foot wide, sending up slender but strong stems, clothed with small, narrow leaves and ending in tall spikes of small bluish-purple snapdragon-like flowers.

There is an equally fine pink form known as 'Canon J. Went', but I have never been able to discover who the Canon was, despite numerous enquiries. If any reader of this book can offer any clues I would be glad to have them. This pink form comes true from seed, incidentally, and although plants may be divided for propagation purposes, it is usually easy to find plenty of self-sown seedlings round the parents. These toadflaxes do not mind a little shade.

Linum (Flax). The herbaceous flaxes, of which there are three, also flower over a long period, the yellow kind, *L. flavum*, seldom being out of flower all summer long. This is a pretty little front-row plant, for a sunny place, or it may be used to help to clothe a sunny bank. It grows to about a foot high. The blue-flowered kinds, *L. narbonnense*, rich deep blue, and *L. perenne*, the sky-blue native flax, grow about $1\frac{1}{2}$ ft and thrive in the same sort of situations. They are usually in flower by late May and bear their blooms continuously over the next couple of months. No special soil is required; they seem to do well enough anywhere.

Loosestrife, Purple. *See under Lythrum.* **Yellow,** *under Lysimachia*

Lupinus (Lupin). To think of lupins immediately makes modern gardeners think of 'Russell Lupins', the marvellous strain developed by the late Mr George Russell over a period of many years and introduced a few years before the last war. These completely transformed the lupin; the colours now vie with the rainbow hues of the iris and for the month of June they are among the glories of the border. Cutting down the stems as soon as flowers have faded, encourages the development of secondary spikes, which flower later in the summer and autumn, but these are never so large and the lupin must be considered a plant of early summer.

As far as varieties go 'you pays your money and you takes your choice'. They are all beautiful, all associate well with one another, and one of the finest sights I have seen was a border 6 ft wide and 40 ft long entirely devoted to Russell lupins all carefully, but unobtrusively staked – which is essential if the heavy spikes are to be kept upright and undamaged by winds and heavy rain.

This border was in a large garden where it did not matter if there was not much to see in that particular border after the lupins were over. Most of us will be content with groups in the herbaceous border, for which they are admirably suited. All grow 3–4 ft tall except the dwarf 'Charmaine', a pleasant terracotta colour.

A word of warning is necessary for those who garden on chalky or limy soils; these plants do not do well there, especially on thin soils overlying chalk. In my present garden I won't even attempt them as the soil is so thin. In my last garden where the soil was somewhat deeper but still over chalk, they

Scabiosa caucasica

Incarvillea delavayi

Tall bearded irises, varieties of *Iris germanica*

Kniphofia uvaria

Russell lupins

Ligularia clivorum

Polygonatum multiflorum, the Solomon's seal

Pyrethrum 'Brenda', bright cerise

Rudbeckia 'Autumn Glow', one of the many fine coneflowers

The horse-chestnut-like leaves of *Rodgersia aesculifolia*

Sidalcea 'Rev. Page Roberts'

Primula viali

Sedum spectabile

Euphorbia epithymoides

grew to a mere 1½–2 ft and looked pretty miserable representatives of a magnificent strain. They do well on other soils, do
not mind partial shade and appreciate a mulch of compost or
something stronger in spring to help them to build up solid
spikes; they must on no account, however, be given fresh
manure.

To propagate named varieties or particular colour forms,
the only sound method is to take cuttings in spring, as described in Chapter 3. Lupins will grow easily from seed
but a batch of seedlings so raised will be a pretty mixed
lot, some good, some bad, some indifferent. Raise them so by
all means but select the seedlings when they are in flower and
throw out the wishy-washy colours and those with poor spikes.

Lychnis (Campion). The wild campions and ragged robins
which add so much colour to our hedgerows and woodlands in
April and May are related to the cultivated lychnis, a relationship which is easy to distinguish from the flowers. They are
delightful, colourful plants although one, the well-known
grenadier-like *L. chalcedonica* with its domed trusses on erect,
3-ft stems in July, is a bit too bright in many places, a really
fiery scarlet, only to be compared with some of the more
dazzling, eye-aching salvia colours.

However, if you can't stand this colour there are other
lychnis. Perhaps the best one is the rose campion, *L. coronaria*,
which has silvery-felted leaves and flowers of deep pink or
crimson. There is a charming white form, *alba;* both flower
from June to September and grow about 2 ft high. They can
be recommended for chalky soils. There are several other
lychnis worth exploring, rather less tall, with flowers in bright
scarlets, pinks and oranges. Increase by division; easy from
seed.

Lysimachia. Three valuable garden plants come under
this heading. To start with the smallest, or rather the shortest,
I must mention our cottage-garden native Creeping Jenny
(*L. nummularia*), although I would not recommend it as a

P.F.G.—5

border plant. It grows about 2 in or so tall and creeps across the ground, making a tangled mass of green leaves, smothered with pretty yellow flowers for most of the spring and summer, especially if it is given a position in moist shade. Even if it is given a particular position it won't stay there long as it will spread rapidly, rooting as it goes. But don't let this deter you from planting it in the right place, for it helps to keep down weeds and provides a pleasant green and yellow carpet. Nature abhors vacant spaces in the soil; such places soon get filled with weeds. It pays therefore to plant something to deny the ground to weeds and for this Creeping Jenny is very useful and decorative. If it gets out of hand it is easy enough to control with the spade and fork.

Lysimachia clethroides is very different; it grows about 2–2½ ft tall, makes a spreading, but not invasive clump, and its strong stems bear from July to September spikes of white flowers. These spikes bend over elegantly, horizontally or below the horizontal and then curve up again at the slender tip, altogether reminiscent of the head and beak of some bird. This plant has the added advantage that its leaves turn pleasant reddish-brown in autumn, thus extending its season of usefulness. It grows well on chalk soils.

Different again is another cottage flower – the 3-ft upright, stiff-stemmed *L. punctata* (*verticillata*). The stems are leafy, the leaves borne in groups of four at right-angles round the stem. From the leaf-axils appear groups of bright yellow, inch-wide flowers, leaves and flowers more crowded towards the top of the stem. This may be a common plant and hardly ranks as an aristocrat of the border, but I for one would not be without it for it grows very well on chalk. It is one of those unfailingly easy plants and it lasts in water surprisingly well, so that it should find its place in the cutting bed when the time comes to divide clumps which is usually after a couple of years as it grows rapidly. These last two lysimachias, which are blood-brothers of our old Yellow Loosestrife (*L. vulgaris*), do well in shade as in sun. All are increased by division.

Lythrum. Although *Lythrum salicaria* is called Purple Loosestrife, it is nothing like Yellow Loosestrife. It is a native plant found in moist, water-side meadows occasionally, which gives a clue to its requirements in the garden – moist shade. It looks magnificent by a stream or pool. It is the selected forms, the rosy-red 'Brightness', the rose-pink 'Prichard's Variety' and the deep crimson 'The Beacon', which are grown in gardens, rather than the reddish-purple native kind. All these grow to about 4 ft and their main flowering period is during July and August.

Another lythrum worth a place is the European *L. virgatum*, in its rosy-red form 'Rose Queen'. This grows to $2\frac{1}{2}$ ft and needs the same conditions as the purple loosestrife.

Macleaya (Plume Poppy). *Macleaya cordata* (often found under the older name *Bocconia cordata*), is one of the most interesting of hardy plants, a real aristocrat, but not, it seems, to everyone's taste. It has a very long season of interest in the garden because of the beauty of its leaves. These are borne fairly sparsely on white or bluish-green stems which on a well-grown plant may soar to 7 or 8 ft. The lower leaves are large, almost a foot wide, round in general outline but pleasantly lobed, silvery-green above, almost white or pinkish-white on the undersides. By contrast the leaves at the top of the tall stems are only about an inch wide and above these appear large, loose plumes of small, airy white or pale buff flowers in July and August, followed by equally airy-looking seed heads. The variety 'Kelway's Coral Plume' grows a little taller and has charming pink plumes.

Despite the height of the stems the macleaya needs little staking except in exposed, windy situations. Deep, rich soil, a sunny place and protection from cold winds are usually re-commended. But it doesn't always pay to go by the book. I heeled in some plants on the north side of the house, on a fairly shallow chalky soil, which had probably not been fed for many years. The garden was 500 ft up, exposed to all the winds that blew – and the north and east winds blew cruelly, even in summer. I can only say that the plants, which by chance were not moved to the border, grew to well over 6 ft for two successive seasons and flowered profusely, although they got little sun after mid morning.

We now grow the plant on even thinner chalky soil. It does not much exceed 4 ft but is still worth its place and I am sure that as we gradually improve the fertility of the soil it will eventually attain its true magnificence.

Meconopsis. These beautiful and aristocratic poppy relatives require special conditions. If you can provide them with a deep, moist, acid soil, enriched with leaf-mould and well-rotted manure if available, then it is worth attempting them. What they really like is a leafy, woodland soil and they often do well in association with rhododendrons and azaleas, in light woodland situations with dappled shade.

These Asiatic poppies fail in many southern gardens, I feel, because the conditions are not cool enough in many summers. They thrive in the cooler, moist air in the north, particularly in Scotland. However, I have seen them doing well in parts of Kent and Surrey where the soil is acid and have grown them on a lightened clay soil, but not on the chalk.

The favourite is undoubtedly the Blue Himalayan Poppy (*Meconopsis betonicifolia*), a 3-ft tall, leafy plant with wide, somewhat nodding saucer-shaped flowers of a wonderful azure blue. This is quite easily raised from seed but seedlings should not be allowed to flower in their first year, otherwise they may die before flowering again. However, seed germinates so easily that the best thing to do is to let a proportion only flower in the first year, pinching out the flower-stems of the remainder as they develop. These will build up strong crowns which will thereafter behave as perennials.

A number of other meconopsis behave in a similar way,

flowering and then dying and I won't mention these here as they are not true perennials. *M. grandis* is a perennial not unlike the Himalayan blue poppy, not quite so tall, and with flowers not as bright blue, often distinctly purplish. The 2-ft tall *M. villosa* has yellow flowers.

Yellow-flowered, too, is *M. cambrica*, the Welsh Poppy, a much less difficult member of the genus, to which my remarks above about soil and other conditions do not apply as it will grow quite easily almost anywhere. It grows about 18 in tall and flowers from May onwards, which is roughly the time when the Asiatic species flower.

Meadow Sweet. See Filipendula
Meadow Rue. See Thalictrum
Michaelmas Daisy. See Aster

Mimulus (Monkey Flower or Musk). This is another excellent little plant for providing ground cover where the soil is moist. We used to grow it near a dripping stand-pipe where the soil was always slightly damp and by the edge of a fish-pool, where boggy soil was provided by storm water. There several kinds flourished, and this is the right word, for they spread and intermingled to cover an area of several square yards, and were a magnificent sight throughout the summer months. Indeed, they should be kept away from more precious plants, which they will quickly throttle.

Excellent kinds are *M. luteus*, the native plant which often reaches 2 ft but is very variable both in height and in the markings on the yellow flowers. These may be 2 in long and usually have variable brownish markings on their throats. In the variety 'A. T. Johnson' the flowers are red spotted. In the hybrid *M. burnetii* the markings reddish-brown or bronze in colour are even more heavy and produce a most attractive effect. In *M. cupreus*, flowers are yellow or coppery.

It is possible also to obtain named varieties such as the crimson 'Red Emperor' and 'Whitecroft Scarlet' which is actually better described as vermilion than scarlet. 'Fireflame' is scarlet, flushed coppery-red and 'Cerise Queen' is described by its name. These plants are dwarfer, growing only to about 6 to 9 in tall.

These musks have the odd habit of producing small resting leaves during the winter months, which lie flat on the surface. Propagation is extremely easy by detaching small pieces of the plant.

Monarda (Bergamot). The normal monarda of gardens *M. didyma*, or Bee Balm, is a plant of striking character, having curiously wrought flowers in whorls that girdle the stem and crown the top. Like the phlox, it will flag in drought and so wants a moisture-retaining soil, with compost and moist peat dug in generously before planting. A position in partial shade also helps.

Monarda didyma looks very well in the border, especially when massed in large groups, for it flowers from late June to September. It is available in a number of named varieties, most of them growing about 3 ft, although the popular cerise-pink 'Adam' scarcely reaches this and the purplish-red 'Sunset' grows taller. Other good varieties include the pink, purplish-leaved 'Beauty of Cobham', 'Cambridge Scarlet' (the most popular), 'Croftway Pink', the crimson 'Mrs. Perry' and the red 'Pillar Box'.

Monkshood. See Aconitum

Nepeta (Catmint). *Nepeta faassenii* is one of the finest of all edging plants both for the border and for other hot, dry, sunny spots in the garden, including banks and the tops of retaining walls. It is most valuable for its long flowering period – from May to September – and for the fact that it needs no staking and little attention. If the border is flanked by a lawn or grass pathway one must hold the growths back when mowing, as they spread over the edge, but this can be done for this and other plants which behave in the same way by making a simple device of pieces of lathing nailed together, the ends pointed, which can be driven into the soil to keep back the sprawling shoots. Catmint has small grey leaves and long spikes of lavender-mauve flowers and it makes a mound about a foot high but considerably more across.

N. mussinii superba is a good deal taller at 3 ft and it has somewhat darker flowers and larger leaves. A pretty variety which is not seen as often as either of these is 'Souvenir d'André Chaudron', which has large lavender-blue flowers, produced later in the summer.

Oenothera (Evening Primrose). The common evening primrose is a biennial and does not conern us here. But there are several perennial kinds, equally beautiful, if not more so. The best is *O. missouriensis* which does not grow more than about 9 in tall but spreads generously with very large flowers of a beautiful soft yellow from about midsummer to late August. The flowers are sometimes spotted with red. This is a fine edging plant for a sunny place and in soil on the rich side.

The sundrop, *O. perennis*, is another pleasant plant, growing to about a foot tall, bearing bright yellow flowers abundantly during the summer. *O. odorata sulphurea* grows about 2–3 ft tall and has wide yellow flowers, up to $2\frac{1}{2}$ in wide, which turn reddish as they age. The leaves and stems, too, are red-tinted. The fragrant flowers open only in the evening which may be a little disadvantage to the stay-at-home gardener, but is not much of a drawback to those who see their gardens only in the evening. The evening primroses do best on the lighter soils but are not really fussy and we have grown them very well both on clay and on thin, poor soils over chalk.

Paeony. The flowering season of paeonies is not a long one, but they are truly magnificent plants and full of interest from the time their rufous shoots appear above the ground in spring, to the time when the last of their heavy flowers falls with an almost audible crash on a July day. Their foliage is also agreeable and an excellent root cover for lilies.

I must say that, much as I admire the double varieties derived from *P. lactiflora*, the so-called 'Chinese' paeonies, there is nothing quite like the old cottage-garden paeonies, the great double varieties of *P. officinalis* with their heavily fragrant flowers. The 'Old Double Crimson', *rubra plena*, the 'Old Double Rose', *rosea plena*, and the 'Old Double White', *albo-plena*, all growing 2 ft tall and flowering in May, have been known in this country for over 400 years. I recall them in our garden when I was a boy and there is still a sense of excitement when the large buds begin to show colour as their green coverings split on a May morning.

As far as the Chinese paeonies go, there is a good choice of colour, as there are probably forty or fifty different varieties in cultivation. They all grow about $2\frac{1}{2}$ ft tall. The colours are mainly in the pink, red, crimson, white range, with few exceptions, including 'Canarie', which, when it first opens is a pale primrose-yellow, but changes to white as it ages. The single forms are equally decorative as they are distinguished by a mass of golden stamens in their centres.

All these paeonies need a rich, moist soil, but do not mind sun or shade; in fact, in shade the colours are less apt to bleach. Once planted, they never need disturbing and will go on for years and years.

To enable them to keep up this display, they should be top-dressed each autumn with a 3–4 in thick layer of a mixture of well-rotted manure and leaf-mould, or compost and leaf-mould. The same material may be used as a spring mulch, particularly on the drier soils, to reduce the necessity for watering in dry weather. When planting in autumn or spring, see that the crown is buried just a couple of inches below the surface, no more.

Papaver (Poppy). Like the paeonies, the Oriental poppies, varieties of *Papaver orientale*, have a short flowering period only, May and June. But they are brilliant while they last and are marred only by their distressing foliage as it decays, which it does very early. Also like the paeonies, they have large buds, hairy in the poppies, which develop over a period of several weeks in the spring, getting larger and larger until they begin to split to reveal the colour of the petals concealed within.

Then suddenly one morning a process which it is possible for the patient gardener to observe, the flower finally opens, and, like a butterfly emerging from its chrysalis, the last vestige of covering is removed and the flower almost visibly struggles out as the green calyx segments fall away. A crumpled beauty, at first, but to continue the analogy, the petals quickly straighten out as do the wings of the butterfly and the flower is fully open, perhaps 8 to 9 in or more across, but destined to last for two or three days only.

Orange is found in several varieties such as 'Lord Lambourne' and 'Marcus Perry', in which it is relieved by a prominent black patch on each petal. Personally I prefer the cerise 'Mrs Stobart', the double 'Salmon Glow' and the wonderful white, black-blotched 'Perry's White'. These poppies grow about 3 ft tall, except for the dwarf, salmon-scarlet 'Peter Pan', which is about a foot tall. Again, these are plants with long, fleshy roots which do not need moving for years; indeed, to move them at all is a considerable feat.

Penstemon. The penstemon is a plant that carries spires of trumpet or tubular flowers, elegantly displayed. Not all are bone hardy, but *P. barbatus*, a 3-ft tall plant may be considered so and is a valuable border plant, as it comes into flower in late summer and often still has a few flowers when practically everything else in the border has ceased to bloom. The tubular blooms are scarlet; there is a form, *coccineus*, in which they have more coral-red in them. 'Garnet' a popular border plant, is a 1½-ft tall hybrid, its flower colour described by its name. *P. schonholzeri*, sometimes known as 'Firebird' is a really bright red. These, too, flower in late summer and early autumn.

FIG. 16. *Penstemon barbatus* is a valuable border plant for late
summer and autumn. It has tubular flowers in scarlet or red

Penstemons are not fussy about soil, provided it is well drained and enriched as it should be for most border plants. They like a sunny place and should be planted in spring rather than autumn, although once established they should survive most winters. Increase by stem cuttings.

Phlox. What George Russell did for the lupin it might be said that Capt. Symons-Jeune did for the herbaceous phlox, except that it was not so much a matter of introducing new colours as of improving the form and size of the truss and the size of the individual flowers. Good varieties of the herbaceous phlox (*P. paniculata*) now have large trusses of overlapping fragrant flowers, giving them a solid appearance, in a beautiful colour range. They include the lavender-blue 'Toits de Paris', the claret-red 'Vintage Wine', 'Lilac Time', the white 'Everest' with a pale heliotrope throat, the mulberry 'Fairy's Petticoat', 'Red Indian', and the peach-pink, crimson-eyed 'Firefly'.

There are many others besides the Symons-Jeune strain; the selection is a matter of personal taste. Heights range from 2–4 ft. All varieties last well when cut. Like the monardas described on p. 102, the border phloxes are very sensitive to dryness in the soil and flag very quickly before most other plants are showing signs of distress. They must have a rich soil with plenty of moisture-retaining material dug in and they seldom do well on a light sandy soil unless it is considerably improved. They do well in partial shade where the soil is usually moister than it is in the sun.

Old plants should be divided every three or four years, using only the younger divisions for propagation purposes. The eelworm disease that attacks phloxes is dealt with in the last chapter.

Pinks. See Dianthus

Physalis (Chinese Lantern). This is one of the few herbaceous plants not grown for the sake of its flowers, which are a dirty white in colour and resemble much-enlarged potato flowers. Instead, they are grown for the brilliant orange-red

FIG. 17. The Chinese Lantern (*Physalis franchetii*) is an example of a plant which is grown not for its flowers but for its seed-pods. These hang like bright orange-red lanterns in the autumn. Cut and brought indoors they can be used to add much colour to vases of dried flowers

inflated calyces which surround the similarly-coloured fruit and hang from the plants like Chinese lanterns in the autumn. Cut and dried at this stage, before wind and weather and slugs get at them, they will last practically for ever. Although we have not grown the plant for about five or six years we occasionally open drawers to find a stem of these lanterns, still retaining their colour, a reminder of the time when we used them in winter vases of dried flowers to brighten up the browns which seem to predominate in such arrangements.

Physalis franchetii is almost too easy to grow; in fact, the problem sometimes is how to get rid of it once one has got it, because every bit of root left in the soil seems to produce a new plant. It grows 2 ft or so tall and, although the usual recommendation is that it should be given a sunny position in a rich soil, it seems to do well enough in part shade and any ordinary garden soil.

Physostegia (Obedient Plant). *Physostegia virginiana*, 'Vivid', is one of the plants which must be grown if the border season is to be extended to its limits for it is seldom in flower until August when flowers are at a premium and goes on flowering until November in an open autumn. It grows about 2 ft tall and bears handsome spikes of bright rose-coloured flowers. The name 'Obedient Plant' refers to the fact that wherever these flowers are moved to on the stem there will they stay, instead of returning to their proper, symmetrical positions on the spike. The plants spread rapidly but not invasively in moist soil in shade or semi-shade. There are other forms available, but 'Vivid' is the best.

Platycodon (Balloon Flower). In its best form, *mariesii*, the Chinese Balloon flower, *Platycodon grandiflorum*, is one of the most handsome of front-row plants for the sunny border. It closely resembles the border campanula. This particular form grows about a foot tall and is more effective because its blue bells are larger, often 2 in wide, than in the parent species. This latter grows about 18 in tall and also has a white-flowered variety, *albus* and a pink form, *roseus*. The name balloon flower comes from the large, curiously-inflated flower buds which develop in June, opening from July onwards. Plants do not seem fussy about soil; we have grown them equally well on chalk and clay.

Polemonium. We grow two polemoniums and can thoroughly recommend them both. One is *P. carneum*, a plant about 18 in tall at the most, which smothers itself with quite large blue flowers in April and May, with odd flowers appearing from time to time throughout the summer. The other is the common Jacob's ladder, *P. caeruleum*, of which the best form is 'Blue Pearl', which is only a foot high but produces its blue flowers equally freely, mainly during May and June. Both plants are quite decorative in foliage as the many leaflets are carried in opposite pairs up the stem (hence 'Jacob's Ladder'). They will grow anywhere and are drought-resistant. Increase by division.

Polygonatum (Solomon's Seal). Fine shade-loving plants, associating well with ferns, doing well under trees, the polygonatums are among those herbaceous plants that look better in a naturalistic surrounding rather than in a formal border. They need no staking; their gracefully arching stems are strong and in *P. multiflorum*, also known as David's Harp, they are about 2½–3 ft tall, or would be if they were upright. Spaced out along the stem, appearing from the leaf axils, hang the white, bell-shaped flowers.

P. officinale, a native plant, is a good deal shorter, about a foot in height, but has similar flowers, although the bells do not open very much at the mouth. The flowering period for both is May and June. They belong to the lily family and as with many others of that family the leaves and stems turn brown and die down fairly quickly after the flowers have faded. For the sake of tidiness cut them off then.

Polygonum (Knot Weed). A genus to treat with a certain amount of caution as some species are very invasive. One can fight a losing battle against *P. cuspidatum*. By far the best knot

FIG. 18. The Jacob's Ladder (*Polemonium caeruleum*) smothers
itself with blue flowers in May and June

weeds for the smaller garden are *P. affine*, *P. amplexicaule* and *P. campanulatum*. *P. affine* is evergreen in many gardens, its low mat of leaves spreading across the soil but not invasively, sometimes turning a beautiful bronze-red in winter. The pink flowers are borne closely packed in 9-in tall spikes in late summer and autumn. Quite the best form is 'Darjeeling Red' as the flowers are a much better colour.

P. amplexicaule is a good deal taller as it may reach 3 ft. The flowers are rosy-red or pinkish white according to variety and are again borne in slender spikes in late summer. By contrast the pretty, blush-pink flowers of *P. campanulatum*, are borne in much looser formation; this is an attractive plant with glaucous foliage.

Poppy. *See Papaver*

Potentilla (Cinquefoil). The cinquefoils suitable for the border are free-flowering plants with leaves like those of the strawberry, to which they are related, and with flower stems which often need a little staking, otherwise they may flop about. They grow about 18 in tall and flower from June to September. They do best on the lighter soils and feeding should not be overdone, otherwise they may run to leaf rather than flower. *P. atrosanguinea*, with crimson flowers, is a good species to grow; otherwise there are named hybrids including 'Gibson's Scarlet', the crimson 'Mons Rouillard', 'White Beauty' and, for those who like orange as a colour, an old variety 'William Rollison', with semi-double, orange-centred flowers.

Primula. This very large and very lovely genus includes the primrose, the cowslip, the oxlip, the polyanthus, the auricula and innumerable plants called simply primula. There are so many to choose from that one hardly knows where to start or to stop. It becomes a little easier if one omits the water-side primulas, but this might limit the selection too much, for there are often places in the small garden, not necessarily by the water-side, where these beautiful creations may be grown. Let us merely say that, given a really moist soil and partial shade, one should not miss the chance of planting some of the 'candelabra' primulas (the name refers to the flowers, borne in tiers up the stem), which are of exceptional grace and beauty.

Among these are the orange-apricot *P. bulleyana*, 2 ft tall, *P. japonica*, 1½ ft tall in reds, pinks and white, the red *P. pulverulenta*, often 3 ft tall, and especially beautiful in the strain known as 'Bartley', and *P. helodoxa*, about the same height, with golden flowers. All these flower in June and July, later than most primulas, and when happy will seed themselves around in the damp soil. They disappear when dormant, so their stations should be labelled.

P. florindae is another impressive water-loving primula, which will even grow where its roots are in shallow water. This flowers about the same time as those described above and may reach 3 ft. It has pale yellow flowers. It associates well with a pretty, but rather odd-looking primula, *P. viali*, which to the uninitiated looks more like a miniature red hot poker or a wild orchid rather than a primrose relative. Its reddish-violet flowers are borne in short tight spikes on stems about 18 in tall.

Not all of us can provide the right conditions for these waterside primulas. But there are plenty of others. For informal situations among lightly-foliaged trees or anywhere rather cool and shady, but not in the formality of a planned border, rotting beats our charming native primrose, *P. vulgaris*. Somewhat more sophisticated than these dryads of the woods are the cultivated 'coloured' primroses, of which 'Blue Queen' is a good strain. There are also double-flowered varieties such as the white *albo-plena* and the reddish mauve 'Marie Grousse' and it is occasionally possible to obtain plants of the 'hose-in-hose' primrose, one perfect flower inside another.

More common are the coloured hybrids of *P. juliae*, especially the familiar claret-purple 'Wanda'; other easy ones are the crimson 'Betty Green' and the roseate 'E. R. Janes'. Less common, but undeservedly so, are the hardy, golden, thick-leaved auriculas, but one must be careful to avoid the alluring

greenhouse varieties. Nor is the charming drumstick primula, *P. denticulata*, whose stems are crowned with orbs of
tiny flowers in lilac, red or white, a difficult plant to grow.

Perhaps the most widely grown of all the *Primula* genus,
however, is the *Polyanthus*, which is a hybrid and carries large
trusses of florets on a thick stem. There are several excellent
strains, of which Blackmore and Langdon's selected blue strain
is justly celebrated. There are strains in gold, white, pink and
parti-colours.

Most of the primulas here mentioned are easily grown from
seed, particularly the polyanthus, though hybrid forms will not
exactly resemble their parents. Multiplication of those that
one likes best is done by splitting up the plants and this should
be done as a regular routine when, especially in the polyanthus,
the plants develop into dense masses.

The charming rock-garden primulas are not within the scope
of this book and few of them are suitable for herbaceous
gardens.

Pulmonaria (Lungwort). One of the pleasanter plant
associations in spring is that of primroses and pulmonarias.
One of these, in particular, *P. officinalis*, is an old cottage-garden plant and has several homely nicknames, including Spotted Dog, Soldiers-and-Sailors and Jerusalem Cowslip. It is an
attractive foliage plant for much of the year, its broad leaves
spotted with white. In spring it bears sprays of flowers which
open pink and then change to blue and, as these open in
succession, it looks as though two differently-coloured flowers
were borne by the same plant.

P. angustifolia, also known as the Blue Cowslip, has the same
engaging habit but its leaves are unspotted. There are also the
red-flowered *P. rubra* and the Bethlehem Sage, *P. saccharata*,
which behaves in much the same way as *P. officinalis* but has
leaves which are more liberally splashed with white.

All these grow about a foot tall and are very easy decorative
little plants. They are generally recommended as shade plants

but do perhaps even better in full sun. Increase by division.

Pyrethrum. Strictly speaking these should take their place with the chrysanthemums for they are derived from *C. coccineum*, but as they are always referred to as pyrethrums they are described here. They are useful plants as they give a brilliant display of flowers in May and June and are among the best of cut flowers. They should be planted in spring, not autumn. They are inclined to look a little untidy unless their long flowering growths are supported by twiggy sticks.

There is an excellent selection of colours in the pink-red range, and some good whites, with single or double flowers. New varieties appear in commerce from time to time but there are many excellent older ones including the pink 'Eileen May Robinson', the crimson 'Harold Robinson' and 'Scarlet Glow'. 'Bressingham Red' is a somewhat newer large-flowered crimson. All these are singles. Good doubles include the white 'Mont Blanc', the crimson 'J. N. Twerdy' and the pink 'Queen Mary'. All varieties grow to about 2½ ft. Cut down all the flower stems when their blooms are over and a second flowering will result.

Ranunculus. To mention the word 'buttercup' to a gardener may be tantamount to waving a red rag at a bull. But ranunculus are cultivated buttercups, even though they are not invasive, which is a very good thing as everyone knows who has had the task of trying to clear a garden of creeping buttercup, especially on a heavy clay soil. For the white-flowered *R. aconitifolius* it is better to use the charming name 'Fair Maids of Kent', and for its double-flowered form, the equally charming name 'Fair Maids of France'. These are pleasant May-flowering plants, both growing to about 2 ft tall or a little less. There is also *R. acris plenus*, which has double, yellow rosettes. All these do best in damper places.

Red Hot Poker. *See Kniphofia*

Rodgersia. The rodgersias are not seen as often as they

might be, possibly because they need a little extra attention. It is worth giving them this for they are good foliage plants and are handsome in flower. The foliage effect is due to size and form of their handsome leaves and they do take up rather a lot of room.

One of the best of them is *R. aesculifolia*, which has large leaves looking very much like those of a horse-chestnut tree. This sends up a 4-ft tall stem, the top 2 ft of which bears clusters of white flowers. There are other species with leaves of similar form, with pink or yellow flowers, but in *R. tabularis*, one of the 'architectural' plants, the rounded leaves, which may be nearly 3 ft in diameter, have the leaf-stalk attached to the centre of the underside, in the same way as a nasturtium leaf. This sends up 3-ft sprays of white flowers.

All these like shade or at least partial shade and a moist soil. Although they are said to do best on the peaty soils I have seen *R. aesculifolia* doing very well, year after year, on a soil which contains much chalk and which was not particularly moist at that. So it may be worth trying for its effect in your garden. It may need some winter protection in very bad weather.

Romneya (Californian Tree Poppy). This is one of the most beautiful of all hardy plants grown in this country. Strictly speaking it is a shrub, but as it is always treated in the same way as herbaceous plants, its stems being cut down in the autumn, I may legitimately include it here. In the warmer counties it is entirely suitable to the back of the herbaceous border, but elsewhere a warm south or west wall is better. The right planting time is spring. *R. coulteri* sends up sturdy stems 4–6 ft tall which in late summer and autumn bear handsome white single poppy-like flowers, often 5 in wide, distinguished by a prominent central ring of golden stamens. The plants spread by runners underground, which travel deeply below the surface, especially in the light sandy soils which the plants prefer. Propagation is by root cuttings taken in January or February.

FIG. 19. Much summer and autumn colour is provided by the
Cone Flowers (Rudbeckias). This is the deep-yellow, dark-
centred *R. deamii*

The romneya often listed as *R. trichocalyx* is virtually the same thing and possibly a little better.

Rudbeckia (Cone Flower). These are also fine daisy-form plants which do much to help to make our borders colourful throughout the summer and autumn. The shorter kinds, growing about 2 to 2½ ft tall, flower in summer and are suitable for centre positions in the border, where they make large plants, flowering very freely. Of these most species have yellow or golden-yellow ray petals with prominent black centres; they include *R. deamii*, *R. speciosa* and *R. sullivantii* 'Goldsturm'. But more colour is provided by the *R. hirta* hybrids, much the same height, with flowers in reds, brownish-reds, oranges, golds and yellows.

Following these, flowering in the autumn, come the tall, back-of-the-border species and varieties, with single or double flowers. The best of the doubles are 'Golden Ball' and 'Golden Glow', the colour in the former being more lemony-gold than pure gold. Both grow about 6 ft tall. The same height is reached by the popular *R. nitida* 'Herbstsonne' in which the flowers have large green conical centres from which the golden petals reflex. Despite its name, *R. maxima* does not quite reach the height of the other tall kinds but is a good plant nevertheless, with yellow flowers and black central cones.

None of these rudbeckias is particular about soil; they have done as well with us on chalk as on heavy clay or loam. But they need a fair amount of staking and tying, particularly in exposed situations.

Salvia (Sage). The brilliant scarlet sages so often seen in summer bedding schemes are half-hardy plants. There are, however, a few hardy sages which are exceptionally good value in the border. Chief among them is the hybrid *Salvia superba*, still often catalogued under its euphonious old name of *S. virgata nemorosa*, a plant for growing in large closely-massed groups when it really deserves the name 'superba'. It grows

FIG. 20. Although *Salvia patens* is not quite hardy and should
be lifted and over-wintered in a frost-free frame, it is well worth
this trouble for the sake of its bright blue flowers

about 2½–3 ft tall and has deep blue flowers surrounded by purple bracts which persist long after the last blue flower has fallen in late summer. There are dwarf forms of this, 'East Friesland' and *lubeca*, both about 18 in tall, but otherwise similar.

Another good sage is *S. haematodes*, which bears light blue flowers in early summer, on stems 3 ft or so tall. Sun and ordinary soil suit all these; they are very easy indeed.

The same is not true, however, of *S. patens*, an exceptionally beautiful plant with Cambridge-blue flowers. This is not hardy and, at the approach of winter, must be lifted and stored in a box of soil, in the same way as the non-hardy chrysanthemums.

Scabiosa (Scabious). Because they flower over such a long period and because they last so well in water when cut, scabious have been among the most important of cut flowers for many years. If you intend to grow them essentially for cutting, it is best to plant them in the kitchen garden or a special cutting bed. They do very well in any ordinary soil, particularly on the chalk. They must be planted in spring rather than autumn, choosing a sunny situation.

Many of us tend to stick to the ever-popular lavender-mauve 'Clive Greaves' without exploring other possibilities. Admittedly the colour range is not very wide, but there *are* variations in the blues, lavender-blues, violet-blues, lilac-blues, powdery-blues, mauves, etc, which are quite noticeable when a number of varieties are grown. Among the best, apart from 'Clive Greaves', are the frilly, mist-blue 'Loddon Anna', the deep blue 'George Souter' and 'Moerheim Blue' and the beautiful white varieties, the older 'Miss Willmott' and the newer 'Loddon White'. All these grow about 2½–3 ft tall, except 'Miss Willmott', which is a little shorter.

Schizostylis (Kaffir Lily). Late-flowering plants are valuable, as they extend the colour season in the garden. One such is the Kaffir Lily, *Schizostylis coccinea*, a South African iris relative with somewhat fleshy roots, which does well in a warm situation, preferably sunny, although the finest clump I have seen was growing in the shade of a large tree on heavy clay soil and I have myself grown good clumps at the foot of a sheltered north wall.

The Kaffir Lily sends up spiky leaves, like those of a gladiolus, and the resemblance is continued in the flowers, which are borne on 18-in stems from September to November. In the ordinary form the flowers are crimson but there are two good varieties, the rose-pink 'Mrs Hegarty' and the pale pink 'Viscountess Byng', which flowers later than the others and does best with cloche protection if required for cutting, not because it is not hardy, but because by late October and November, when it is in flower, the weather has usually deteriorated so much that the flowers are badly battered by autumn gales. In colder gardens some winter protection with bracken is desirable.

Sea Holly. *See Eryngium*

Sea Lavender. *See Limonium*

Sedum. Most of the sedums are rock-garden plants but there are two fine plants for the border. One is *S. maximum atropurpureum*, which may reach 18 in and is remarkable for its mahogany-hued, fleshy stems and leaves, topped in late summer by flattish heads of pink flowers. This is a very handsome sedum, but it is liable to be pillaged by the flower arranger.

The other one is the familiar *S. spectabile*, known to most people as the Ice Plant, an old cottage-garden type plant, but none the worse for that. It makes an equally neat display, 15 in tall, with pale-green, fleshy leaves and pale-pink flowers in flat clusters. There are better varieties, however, such as 'Brilliant', 'Carmen' and 'Meteor', which have flowers of deeper pink or carmine, all flowering in August and September and all attracting the late-summer butterflies, as much as buddleias attract those about in the garden earlier in the summer. Cultivation is very easy; provided they have sun, these sedums are

FIG. 21. Ice Plant is a familiar name for *Sedum spectabile*, the pale pink flowers of which are attractive to the late summer butterflies

as tough as old boots. As they are succulent plants, they survive droughts where other plants suffer. Cut down the stems in autumn; the plants form small resting leaves on the surface of the soil. Then is the time to dig up pieces for propagation.

Senecio. Most of the herbaceous plants (apart from the well-known shrubs) which used to be called senecios are now ligularias, but of those that remain one at least is an excellent but seldom-seen border plant. This is *Senecio tanguticus*, a handsome plant both in leaf and flower, easy to grow and well worth its place as something out of the ordinary, where there is room to spare. It grows easily to 6 ft, sometimes more, and has large, deeply-cut leaves and, in September, massive but airy-looking pyramidical spikes of small golden-yellow flowers.

Even when these fall the interest is not over for fluffy seedheads appear, looking somewhat bedraggled in the early mornings after autumn dews or rains, but fluffing out as they dry and then looking very handsome. This senecio seems to grow in any kind of soil, even quite poor ones, overlying chalk and is not particular about situation, putting up a good show in shade. It has thick, fleshy roots and is inclined to spread but I would not call it a ramper, as it is easy to control.

Solidago (Golden Rod). If *Senecio tanguticus* cannot be classed as a real ramper, the older golden rods certainly deserve to be. They were quite capable of taking over a garden completely and for that reason they dropped from favour. However, the genus is staging a come-back, because in the last few years some fine hybrids have been introduced which are less tall and lack the spreading tendencies usually associated with golden rod.

Such kinds as 'Golden Gates' and 'Golden Mosa', both 2 ft or so tall, are excellent plants, flowering in succession from July to September. The bright yellow 'Lesden' is a little taller; 'Lereft' bears its flowers in bunches rather then in plumes or sprays; 'Lemore' has flattish heads of primrose-yellow flowers, a breakaway from the usual golden-yellow.

The tallest of these newer kinds is the large-flowered 'Golden Wings', a late-flowering plant, in bloom with the majority of the Michaelmas daisies, and associating well with them at the back of the border as it reaches 6 ft when well grown. By contrast, it is possible to grow one golden rod at least at the front of the border. This is the 15-in tall 'Wendy'. None of these is at all difficult; ordinary soil and a position in sun or partial shade will suit them well. They last well as cut flowers and are increased by division.

Solomon's Seal. *See Polygonum*

Speedwell. *See Veronica*

Spurge. *See Euphorbia*

Stachys (Lamb's Ear or Lamb's Tongue). The purplish-pink flowers of *Stachys lanata*, which appear in July and August, can be discounted; the plant is grown for its remarkable greenish-grey-white leaves and stems and it is well worth growing for these alone, especially to cool down the hotter colours of some flowers. The leaves, large and tongue-shaped, look just as though they might have been cut out of thick felt, so closely covered are they with hairs. The equally hairy flower stems, bearing small leaves, are about 18 in high and one usually removes them.

The plant will spread slowly across the ground, eventually covering quite a large area. In time one gets tired of seeing such a large expanse and chops away to reduce it. Lamb's Ear is a tough plant, surviving many degrees of frost, putting up with heavy rain which does not spoil its appearance for long, growing in poor soils, in sun or part shade. Oddly enough, one of the best of all reasons for growing it is that the stems last for ages in water and look wonderful when arranged with bright summer flowers.

Sunflower. *See Helianthus*

Thalictrum (Meadow Rue). Few garden plants look so airily delicate as the meadow rues, with their dainty flowers

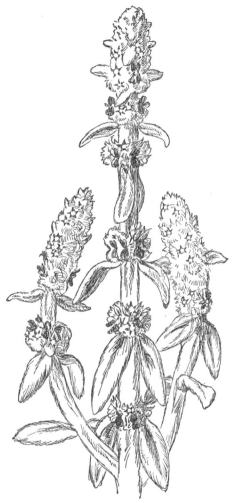

FIG. 22. The woolly flower stems of Lamb's Ear (*Stachys lan-ata*) are sometimes removed and the plant treated as a foliage plant for the sake of its thick felty leaves. But the stems with their small purplish flowers last well in water

nodding on slender stalks and looking as though the slightest puff of wind would blow them away. Yet they are as tough and as hardy as any plant and their wiry stems seldom need staking. *T. aquilegifolium*, so called because its foliage is very like that of the aquilegias, grows to about 4 ft tall and flowers from late May to July. It has small, fluffy, pale purple flowers, borne in a large, conspicuous head. The aptly-named 'Purple Cloud' is a dwarf form of this, with reddish-purple flowers.

The meadow rue more usually grown, however, and more attractive too, is *T. dipterocarpum*, a good deal taller, reaching in its form *magnificum* between 5 and 6 ft. Its tiny lavender-and-yellow flowers hang separately instead of being bunched together in a cloud-like formation. There is a fine white-flowered form, *album*, and an old double-flowered form, known as 'Hewitt's Double', which is somewhat less graceful, but still a fine plant.

To succeed with *dipterocarpum* and its forms, one needs a rather light but rich moist soil, well drained, and therefore an abundant dressing of peat is helpful; it also appreciates light, dappled shade. It should be planted in spring.

Thrift. *See Armeria*

Tradescantia (Spiderwort). The garden spiderworts, all growing about 18 in tall, are oddly attractive plants with narrow leaves and clusters of large three-petalled flowers, opening in long succession. They are all varieties of *Tradescantia virginiana*, a plant introduced from Eastern America over three hundred years ago. There is nothing spectacular about it and the heavy foliage is out of scale to the rather small flowers, but I would not be without it in the border as it is an easy hardy perennial, flowering over a long period, with a charm all its own. About a dozen varieties are in cultivation; among the best are the light blue J. C. Weguelin, the violet-purple 'Purple Dome' the pink *rosea* and the dark red *rubra*. Among the best of several white-flowered kinds is 'Osprey', distinguished by its blue stamens. These spiderworts grow well in sun or partial

Fig. 23. The Spiderwort (*Tradescantia virginiana*) flowers over
a long period during summer and autumn. There are varieties
with flowers in shades of blue, purple, dark red, pink and white.
They do well in town gardens

shade and do not mind the often poor soil found in town gardens.
Increase by division (very tough).

Trollius (Globe Flower). These moisture-loving plants
look best when massed in reasonably large clumps or groups,
towards the front of the border, for they grow about 1½–2 ft
tall. They are among the early plants to flower in the border,
one at least, 'Earliest of All' beginning to produce its lemon-
yellow globular flowers in late April. The season is quite long,
however, for *T. ledebourii*, grown in its form 'Golden Queen',
descriptive of the colour, is in flower in July. They are all excellent for cutting, and, although it is usually recommended
that they are planted in partial shade, I have seen them planted
by the thousand in an open field in full sun for the cut-flower
trade.

Veronica (Speedwell). Plants with their flowers in tall
slender spikes are useful to contrast with some of the larger-
flowered ones such as the border daisies of which there are so
many. *Veronica spicata* and its varieties, flowering from June
onwards throughout most of the summer, are excellent for this
purpose, especially the 2-ft tall 'Pavane', a deep-pink variety,
slightly taller than the others which normally grow to about
1½ ft. Other good kinds include the deep blue 'Crater Lake', the
white *alba*, the pink 'Minuet' and the dwarf rosy-pink 'Bar-
carolle'. All of these make quite extensive colonies when properly established, sending up a multitude of handsome spikes,
closely packed with flowers. They prefer a sunny position but
do not mind if they are partially shaded by nearby taller plants.
Increase by division.

PLANTS FOR SPECIAL PURPOSES

(Botanical names are given first to enable the descriptions of the plants in Chapter 5 to be consulted easily.)

For Shade or Half-Shade

Acanthus (Bear's Breech)
Aconitum (Monkshood)
Anemone hupehensis ⎫ (Japanese Anemones)
Anemone japonica ⎭
Aquilegia (Columbine)
Aruncus sylvester (Goat's Beard)
Astilbe
Bergenias
Brunnera macrophylla (Giant Forget-me-Not)
Campanulas (Bellflowers)
Cimicifugas (Bugbanes)
Dicentras (Bleeding Hearts)
Echinaceas (Purple Cone Flowers)
Geranium endressii (Cranesbill)
Helleborus (Christmas Rose, Lenten Rose, etc.)
Hemerocallis (Day Lilies)
Iris sibirica
Ligularias
Lysimachia
Lythrum salicaria (Purple Loosestrifes)
Meconopsis betonicifolia (Blue Poppy)

Monardas (Bergamots)
Phlox
Platycodons (Balloon Flowers)
Primulas
Pulmonarias (Lungworts)
Ranunculus aconitifolius
Rodgersias
Solidagos (Golden Rods)
Thalictrums (Meadow Rues)
Veronicas (Speedwells)

For Cut Flowers
(see also Chapter 4)

Achilleas (Yarrows)
Alstroemerias (Peruvian Lilies)
Anthemis tinctoria (Golden Marguerite)
Aquilegias (Columbines)
Asters (Michaelmas Daisies)
Campanula glomerata (Bellflower)
Campanula persicifolia (Peach-leaved Bellflower)
Catananche caerulea (Cupid's Dart)
Cephalaria tatarica (Giant Scabious)
Chrysanthemum maximum (Shasta Daisy)
Chrysanthemum leucanthemum (Ox-eye Daisy)
Chrysanthemum rubellum varieties
Chrysanthemums (outdoor varieties generally)
Coreopsis (Tickseed)
Curtonus paniculatus (Aunt Eliza)
Delphiniums
Dianthus (Border Pinks and Carnations)
Dictamnus albus (Burning Bush)
Doronicums (Leopard's Banes)
Echinaceas (Purple Cone Flowers)
Echinops (Globe Thistle)

Erigerons

Eryngiums (Sea Hollies)

Gaillardias

Galegas (Goat's Rues)

Geranium grandiflorum (Cranesbill)

Gypsophilas

Heleniums

Helianthus (Perennial Sunflowers)

Heliopsis (Orange Sunflower)

Helleborus (Christmas Roses, Lenten Roses, etc.)

Iris germanica varieties (Flag or German Irises)

Iris foetidissima (Gladdon or Gladwyn Iris) (colourful seed-
heads)

Liatris

Limoniums (Sea Lavender, Statice)

Linaria purpurea (Purple Toadflax)

Lysimachia punctata

Monardas (Bergamots)

Nepetas (Catmints)

Paeonias

Phlox

Physalis (Chinese Lanterns) (inflated seed capsules in autumn)

Polygonatum (Solomon's Seal)

Primula polyantha (Polyanthus)

Pyrethrums

Ranunculus aconitifolius

Rudbeckias (Cone Flowers)

Salvia superba

Scabiosa caucasica (Scabious)

Schizostylis coccinea (Kaffir Lily)

Sedums

Senecio tanguticus

Solidagos (Golden Rods)

Stachys lanata (excellent cut foliage)

Thalictrums (Meadow Rues)

Trollius (Globe Flowers)
Veronicas (Speedwells)

Many of the above may be cut and dried for winter decoration. Some will provide decorative seed-heads as well as flowers. A few may be used for foliage effect.

For Town Gardens

Aconitums (Monkshoods)
Alstroemerias (Peruvian Lilies)
Anemone japonica ⎫
Anemone hupehensis ⎭ Japanese Anemones
Anthemis (Golden Marguerite)
Aquilegias (Columbines)
Armerias (Thrifts)
Asters (Michaelmas Daisies)
Bergenias
Coreopsis (Tickseed)
Dicentras (Bleeding Hearts, etc.)
Doronicums (Leopard's Banes)
Erigerons
Geums
Heucheras
Iris germanica varieties (Flag or German Irises)
Kniphofias (Red-hot Pokers)
Solidagos (Golden Rods)
Tradescantias (Spiderworts)

The above plants will do quite well in towns where the atmosphere is polluted with industrial smoke. There are many more which will put up a good show in towns where the atmosphere is cleaner.

CHAPTER VI

PESTS AND DISEASES

THIS, fortunately, is almost the shortest chapter in the book. Hardy perennials, on the whole, are not attacked by many garden enemies. It is perfectly feasible for the gardener who does not want to bother with spraying or dusting plants with insecticides or fungicides to do without using either. In most seasons his plants will suffer little damage but occasionally a few plants are badly attacked by pests or such diseases as mildews and then it is best to take some retaliatory action both to prevent damage and to prevent the spread of the trouble.

Slugs

The worst pests of all are not insects, but slugs of one kind or another. A report issued not long ago by the Henry Double-day Research Association shows that the slug population in a garden is probably 300,000 per acre at the minimum and may be very much more. The total weight of slugs may be 180–300 lb per acre and each slug will eat 30–40 times its own weight of food. This is enough to make the keen gardener feel a sense of despair, for obviously it is impossible to deal with such a vast army of slugs. Even if one succeeded in killing all those in one's own garden, more would come in from outside, so we have to face the fact that any battle we fight with slugs is likely to be a losing one.

However, there is a brighter side to the picture. Although

they will eat almost anything, from one's prize seedlings to the slug-bait thoughtfully provided for them by the gardener, their main diet is rubbish, decaying vegetable and animal matter, so it looks as though they do serve a useful purpose as scavengers and that it would be unwise to attempt their complete annihilation.

This being so, it seems as though defence against slugs might well be limited to trying to preserve from their depredations such things as seedlings and the newly-developing shoots of plants in the spring, since they appear to number these among their favourite dishes. Delphinium shoots and Bleeding Heart, in particular, are attacked and iris leaves are often badly damaged, leaving them looking as though the outer part of the leaf has been scraped off. There are various proprietary slug-baits which may be used, mainly based on metaldehyde, or crushed meta fuel may be mixed with moist-tea-leaves, bran, shredded lettuce leaves, or other organic material, and placed in heaps round the plants, protected from the weather by pieces of slate or tile. However, these metaldehyde baits suffer from the drawback that the dead slugs may be eaten by birds or hedgehogs, with possibly fatal results. Moreover, the bait has to be renewed after heavy rain.

Baits not based on metaldehyde are available; I have not tried them. There remains hand-picking, a slightly gruesome job best done after dusk, armed with a bucket of salt water into which the slugs may be dropped. Hundreds may be collected in this way each night. The trouble is that more hundreds will be there the following night and on succeeding nights so that inevitably one gives in and gives the slugs best or calls it a drawn game.

Aphis

A few plants are sometimes attacked by aphis (greenfly, blackfly, and some of other colours). Since they feed by sucking the sap, usually from newly-developing leaves and tender-growing points, they can cause a good deal of damage, causing leaves to curl and become distorted and growth to become stunted through injury to the growing points. The remedies are to spray or dust with derris or pyrethrum-based insecticides as soon as the first signs of attack appear, before a large concentration can be built up. The retaliatory measures may have to be repeated at intervals of 10–14 days, as almost inevitably some pests are missed, however careful one is to wet the undersides of the leaves and force the insecticide into the growing points. Nicotine sprays may be used without the risk of injury to birds but they are not effective unless the temperature is above 64° F. as the effect is partially dependent upon the volatilisation of the material.

Cuckoo-spit

The familiar frothy 'cuckoo-spit' which appears on many border plants in May and June, conceals the yellowish-green larva of an insect pest known as the common frog hopper. This can do a certain amount of damage when the infestation is heavy as it sometimes is on certain plants. The pest may be controlled by spraying the plants forcefully with clear water to wash off the froth. This will not wash off the insect which clings to the plant, but its protection removed it may be dealt with by dusting or spraying with derris or pyrethrum.

Alternatively, you may deal with them with your fingers.

Earwigs

Late summer usually brings plagues of earwigs, often as annoying in the house as in the garden as it is not uncommon to open a window and see scores of these insects scuttling away in all directions, fleeing from the light, as they are nocturnal creatures, hiding away by day in narrow cracks and crevices. The grower of chrysanthemums and dahlias has more cause to fear these insects than the gardener growing hardy herbaceous plants. Trapping in hay-filled inverted flower-pots stuck on canes or in lengths of corrugated paper rolled up and with an elastic band round them, is one method of getting rid of numbers of them, but not only does this involve emptying the traps each day, tipping the insects into a bucket of water to drown, but it scarcely touches the fringes of the problem where the attack is severe, for thousands of insects may be involved. One may either admit defeat or spray with an insecticide containing both derris and pyrethrum, which seems to be more effective than either substance alone.

Other Pests

Other pests that may be a nuisance are those that inhabit the soil. These include the repulsive, bloated larvae of the various chafers, which eat roots, the caterpillar-like cutworm, which nibbles off the tender shoots of young plants at ground level, the brown, tough-skinned, sluggish millipede, the wire worm and the fat, torpid, dirty leatherjacket. As a protection against them, it pays to fork into the top 4 in of soil whizzed or flaked naphthalene at the rate of 2 to 4 oz per square yard.

Border phlox are occasionally damaged by a pest called the stem eelworm, causing the leaves to become distorted and the plants stunted. There is no amateur cure for this; plants should be dug up and burned. They may, however, be propagated from root cuttings (see Chapter III) which will not be affected by the pest and the plants so produced will be healthy. Even so they should not be planted in the same positions for some years as the eelworms will still be present in the soil.

Mildews and Rusts

Mildews and rusts, of which there are various forms, are fungal diseases which occasionally attack plants, especially in warm, damp summers. Michaelmas daisies are particularly prone to attack by a powdery mildew which makes leaves and stems appear grey. Both mildews and rusts may be controlled sufficiently to make their effects negligible by dusting or spraying with a copper or sulphur fungicide, following the manufacturer's instructions. Michaelmas daisies are less prone to attack if their stems are drastically thinned in spring, which also has the desirable effect of inducing them to produce larger flowers more characteristic of the variety.

APPENDIX

Some Nurseries supplying Herbaceous Plants

You will probably find that there is a nursery in your district from which you may obtain a fair range of hardy herbaceous perennials. But for the less common kinds you may have to send away to nurseries which specialise in growing these plants. The following nurseries are a few of those which grow a wide range of these plants; there are many others, which space alone prevents me from listing here.

Bakers (Codsall) Ltd., Codsall, Staffs.

Thomas Carlile Ltd., Loddon Nurseries, Twyford, Berks.

Gayborder Nurseries, Melbourne, Derbyshire.

Hillier & Sons Ltd., Winchester, Hants.

George Jackman & Sons Ltd., Woking Nurseries, Woking, Surrey.

Kelway & Sons Ltd., Langport, Somerset.

Perry's Hardy Plant Farm, Enfield, Middlesex

Maurice Prichard & Sons, Christchurch, Hants.

John Scott & Co., The Royal Nurseries, Merriott, Somerset.

Sunningdale Nurseries, Windlesham, Surrey.

John Waterer, Sons, & Crisp Ltd., The Floral Mile, Twyford, Berks.

Seeds of many hardy herbaceous plants are obtainable from Thompson & Morgan Ltd., Seed Merchants, Ipswich, Suffolk.

Northern Nurseries. A list of these is given in Mr Kenneth Lemmon's *Gardening in the North*, in this series.

INDEX

References in italic type indicate illustrations in the text

These are PAN PIPER Books

THE SMALL GARDEN SERIES
Edited by C. E. Lucas Phillips

The first four volumes in this outstanding new series:

ROSES FOR SMALL GARDENS
C. E. Lucas Phillips (*Illustrated*)

SHRUBS AND TREES FOR SMALL GARDENS   Christopher Lloyd (*Illustrated*)

GARDENING IN THE NORTH
Kenneth Lemmon (*Illustrated*)

PERENNIAL FLOWERS FOR SMALL GARDENS   Peter Hunt (*Illustrated*)

Other titles in preparation. *All priced 5/-*

Books for the taste of today